JEREMY PANG'S SIMPLE FAMILY FEASTS

SCHOOL OF WOK

hamlyn

To my dearest wife Dee, for foregoing our precious evenings together, and to the TV for filling in my husband gap while I've been writing into the morning. To my kids Theo and Rosa, thank you for your patience, and for waiting weeks on end for me to find the time to take you to the park! And to my sisters, my mum and my late dad for providing all those unforgettable feasting moments while I was growing up.

First published in Great Britain in 2023 by Hamlyn, an imprint of
Octopus Publishing Group Ltd
Carmelite House
50 Victoria Embankment
London EC4Y 0DZ
www.octopusbooks.co.uk

An Hachette UK Company
www.hachette.co.uk

Text copyright © Jeremy Pang 2023
Design and layout copyright © Octopus Publishing Group 2023

Distributed in the US by Hachette Book Group 1290 Avenue of the Americas, 4th and 5th Floors, New York, NY 10104

Distributed in Canada by Canadian Manda Group, 664 Annette Street, Toronto, Ontario, Canada M6S 2C8

ISBN 978-0-60063-777-6

A CIP catalogue record for this book is available from the British Library.

Printed and bound in Malaysia

10 9 8 7 6 5 4 3 2 1

Publisher: Eleanor Maxfield
Senior Editor: Pauline Bache
Art Director: Jaz Bahra
Senior Production Manager: Allison Gonsalves

Consultant Editor: Adrienne Katz Kennedy
Designer: Smith & Gilmour
Illustrator: Freya Deabill
Photographer: Kris Kirkham
Food Stylists: Gil Salter, Yasmin Othman and Nicole Herft
Props Stylist: Morag Farquhar
Copy Editor: Jo Richardson

Cook's Notes:
Standard level spoon measurements are used in all recipes.
1 tablespoon = one 15ml spoon
1 teaspoon = one 5ml spoon

Both imperial and metric measurements have been given in all recipes. Use one set of measurements only and not a mixture of both.

Fresh herbs should be used unless otherwise stated. If unavailable, use dried herbs as an alternative but halve the quantities stated.

Oven temperatures are for fan ovens. To adjust for a conventional oven, increase the temperature by 20°C (70°F).

This book includes dishes made with nuts and nut derivatives. It is advisable for customers with known allergic reactions to nuts and nut derivatives and those who may be potentially vulnerable to these allergies, such as babies and children with a family history of allergies, to avoid dishes made with nuts and nut oils. It is also prudent to check the labels of pre-prepared ingredients for the possible inclusion of nut derivatives.

All serving sizes are for a full meal unless otherwise stated. When building several dishes together into a feast please reconsider serving sizes according to how many dishes you are cooking.

CONTENTS

FAMILY FEASTS

If I were a purist, I would be constantly scolding myself for shunning every bit of established eating etiquette, but in the Pang household that's just not how we roll. Growing up, feasting was an everyday ritual, but with two hungry sisters and a constant influx of random family friends joining us for last-minute dinners, there was no time to be polite at the table. We were taught that the biggest respect we could give the food was to get stuck in while it was piping hot, especially if it was a freshly stir-fried lobster, whole steamed fish or crispy chicken that would lose its crispiness with every additional minute that it waited on the plate. And by immediately tucking in, we were also honouring the skills of the chef. I can recall my dad's pride when he arrived at the table, just after serving up the last plateful, to find only a little of his showstopper dish left for him to add to his rice bowl – he saw our frenzied attack on his food as the most sincere form of appreciation.

Chopsticks are ideal for such occasions as these, not just because they are fun to use but because their length helps you to reach for whatever you want from across the table. However, if there's one bit of dining etiquette I do hold to, it's this: don't double dip with your chopsticks! If you haven't got any spare serving chopsticks, then either ask your guests to turn their chopsticks upside down to use the other end to load up their bowls or provide each dish with a large serving spoon or two so that it's easier for everyone to pounce on the meal.

Feasting is ingrained in Asian eating culture no matter what part of the continent you look towards. A spoonful of noodles or a clump of sticky rice perched on the end of your chopsticks are seen as the foundation from which to create a variety of combinations — perfectly placed to mop up the silky, sweet, salty, savoury sauces from steaming hot flakes of fish or melt-in-the-mouth morsels of slow-braised meat. Asian food is able to entice both the taste buds and the mind, and this, the latest School of Wok cookbook, is ready to do just that.

Drawing inspiration from each main culinary tradition and practice found across the continent, chapter by chapter, this book presents a wide variety of dishes for coaxing out the feeders among you to delight family and friends, with the caveat that each dish will work equally well served on their own with a bowl of rice or noodles. In addition to practical tips and tricks to enable you to explore the world of Asian cuisine in new and adventurous ways, the book will help you to build your confidence in preparing multiple dishes at a time and, before you know it, you'll be filling your table with simple family feasts that everyone will want to devour and revisit again and again, creating a secondary feast of memories to nourish your soul.

Of course, half the battle of serving more than one dish, or one dish with several components, is making sure each item is presented at its ideal temperature, with hot dishes presented piping hot while salads are kept chilled and crisp, to provide that refreshing crunch in between the chopstickfuls of rice. This is where my section on Building a Feast (see pages 6–8) and The Feasting Wheel (see pages 7–9) will prove invaluable in guiding you through planning your cooking.

Entertaining the Asian way is not just a matter of cooking a recipe and plonking a plate of the food in front of your guests, so as the host, once you've cooked up your feast, make sure you keep on serving your guests after allowing them to help themselves – you will be amazed at how rewarding this generosity of care will feel. Serving and sharing the results of your hard graft in the kitchen with others in a genuine, unpretentious way can provide a deep sense of fulfilment, as well as creating memorable moments for everyone around the table. So let's get stuck in!

THE WOK CLOCK

The Wok Clock is such a simple and practical way of helping home cooks to be super-organized in their kitchen that it has found its way into cooking demonstrations across the world, besides being referenced all over the internet and talked about in almost every TV show I have been lucky enough to participate in. And I'm pretty sure it'll follow me way past my retirement.

Essentially, at School of Wok, we like to arrange our prepared ingredients in a systematic manner, using a round plate as a Wok Clock. This approach is not exclusive to wok cooking; it's an incredibly useful tool for all types of home cooking. Once you have prepared all your ingredients, arrange them around the plate in the order in which you'll need them, beginning at 12 o'clock and working your way around the plate, clockwise. Whether you're making a stir-fry or a slower-cooked curry, or even setting up a long list of ingredients that need to be pounded using a pestle

and mortar at a particular point in the preparation process, it 'woks' well!

Where appropriate in this book, the Wok Clock approach has been used as a simple guide to preparation so that you're ready to proceed with the recipe in an organized way. Once you get into the habit of using the Wok Clock method, you'll find that every aspect of your cooking will become more straightforward and efficient, freeing you up to relish the joys of preparing dishes and whole feasts and learning new cooking techniques rather than having to painstakingly consult every last sentence of the recipe. Once you have tried a few recipes, you can simply refer to the illustrated Wok Clocks to help you 'wok' your way through without having to over-analyse a recipe every time you decide to cook something new. 'Wok's' not to love? (OK, I'll stop now.)

BUILDING A FEAST

There's so much more to Asian cuisine than just cooking one dish at a time. So here's how to up your game and get organized enough to cook like a traditional Asian aunty or uncle might and present a combination of dishes for everyone to share. When cooking a feast at home, however simple or complex, finding a balance of flavour, colour and texture throughout the dishes you put together is essential. Although taking into account these different factors can feel a bit daunting at the outset, once you achieve a balance of these three key elements, you'll succeed in creating a feast that you and your family and friends won't be able to resist. Great for cooking accolades, bad for leftovers, as everyone will be digging in until the very last morsel of food has been devoured!

Flavour Balance: This is really just the beginning when it comes to nailing that moreish result. The flavours of the base ingredients and sauces set the scene and provide direction for the rest of the dish. In Asian cuisine we aim to reach every part of the palate, utilizing all our taste buds to create a journey through sweet, sour, salty, spicy, savoury and, last but equally important, bitter. There's a certain skill in knowing which recipes to choose to complement each other and create a natural balance of all these flavours when eaten together.

Colour Balance: As we always say at School of Wok: 'feast with your eyes', and this means making your selection of food, whether presented as a single plate or a mix of dishes, aesthetically pleasing. Fortunately, this is easy to achieve in Asian cuisine, as if you've picked the right balance of elements or dishes in terms of the other two main categories of flavour and texture, it's likely that you'll naturally end up with a beautiful array of colours on the table.

Texture Balance: This aspect is often overlooked and slightly more difficult to explain but crucial to elevating a feast from a random selection of dishes to something irresistible, because truly satisfying food is just as much about its texture as its flavour. When considering texture, simply follow the same principle as balancing flavour and ask yourself the question: how can you reach every part of the palate with varying textures? Crispy, fluffy, a gentle bite, chewy, pillowy soft, flaky, slippery, tongue-numbing, drying and melt-in-the-mouth all come to mind, yet they are just a few of the vast dictionary of descriptive terms for food texture. Once you start looking at all these different textural qualities, you'll find that they closely correspond to the key cooking techniques within East and South East Asian cuisines. On page 9 you'll find a breakdown of each major texture featured in this book: Juicy & Succulent, Crunchy, Silky & Melt-in-the-Mouth, A Gentle Bite and Crispy.

THE FEASTING WHEEL

As you may have deduced from my dedication to the Wok Clock, I love the very nature of circles or spheres, the most perfectly uniform and continuous of shapes, and I am of the belief that every good thing is round for a reason: life, our planet, a football, the perfect droplet of stock or soy sauce skittering across an extremely hot pan...So, I'd like to present another round of goodness, the Feasting Wheel – a wheel of foodie fortune to help you cook up a feast for your whole family or group of friends with ease. I invite you to take a glimpse into my brain to understand how my mind figures out exactly what to put on the dinner table.

Think of the Feasting Wheel as a multifaceted pie chart of balance and organization where I have already done the hard work in planning the preparation and cooking of a feast for you. Taking into account texture balance and cooking techniques, the Feasting Wheel will help you devise your plan of action for cooking two or more dishes for a mini family feast or a full-on banquet for your friends.

Each of the chapters in this book (apart from Desserts) presents a range of dishes within each type of Asian cuisine that in combination constitute a well-balanced feast. In the introduction to each chapter I will give you guidance on how to approach each feast, and talk you through the Feasting Wheel for that particular cuisine – see page 9 where

I use the Feasting Wheel from the Chinese chapter to illustrate how the dishes complement each other in detail.

To begin your feasting journey, however, I recommend picking out individual dishes that you would like to make for a midweek meal or a home-cooked treat, and gain experience cooking one dish at a time. Then, following the order of the wheel, you can start to add a salad or a side and build up to tackling several dishes at a time while keeping yourself organized and maintaining enough space on your hob, free from undue fuss and stress. For example, once your roasting dish is in the oven with a timer on to check or baste at the appropriate stage, you can get the slow cooking underway, such as braising or making a nice saucy curry. And while that's simmering, there's plenty of time to prepare and finish off the quicker dishes that will add that essential crisp or crunch to your feast. As with the Wok Clock, I recommend starting at 12 o'clock and, depending on which dishes you have selected, working your way clockwise around the segments of the wheel in organizing your order of preparation. By starting small, such as picking one main dish and a salad, and then adding an extra dish each time you cook from that chapter, you'll soon find it much easier to put more dishes on the table all at once.

Instinctively, you might think that the last item to prepare for each feast would be the salad. But it's important to remember that the best way to present any meal is to ensure that any dishes that need to be hot are served as piping hot as possible, and any dishes that require quick cooking are tackled in the final 10–15 minutes. Therefore, when it comes to salads and other uncooked dishes, these should be prepared when you have a pocket of free time and then stored in the fridge to keep fresh so that you can focus on the last-minute touches of your feast when your guests arrive.

Do note however that, even as a professional chef, I would rarely attempt to cook all eight dishes of any chapter in one go! Rather, I would max out at around four or five to avoid doubling up on similar textures or overstressing when cooking at home. Just remember, always try to include the crunchy veg dish no matter how big or small your feast, so that the larger and heartier dishes don't overload the palate.

I hope you enjoy your cooking journey and adventures as much I have enjoyed creating this book for you. Have fun 'wokking' around your clocks, feast away and I look forward to seeing all your attempts and triumphs!

TEXTURE TIPS

Throughout the book, each of the main textures (Juicy & Succulent, Crunchy, Silky & Melt-in-the-mouth, A Gentle Bite and Crispy) are represented by icons both on the Feasting Wheels and on the individual recipes. This should help you to quickly get the measure of each dish and aid your decision-making in composing your own simple feasts. Although some recipes will provide more than one texture, I have focused on the most prominent texture of each dish to make things as straightforward as possible. Also bear in mind that each recipe works as a stand-alone dish and doesn't have to be prepared alongside any others – the Feasting Wheel and texture icons are merely there to guide you if and when you feel adventurous enough to tackle cooking more than one dish at a time.

Juicy & Succulent: Marinated meats, fish and vegetables will hold their shape and keep their natural succulence and flavoursome juices when roasted or stir-fried.

 Crunchy: These fresh and cool additions to a meal are usually provided by salads and sides, which act as a bridge between flavour and texture, or a refresher from one bite to the next, allowing you to cleanse your palate in between mouthfuls. But crunch and bite can come from main dishes too.

Silky & Melt-in-the-Mouth: Smooth, creamy sauces and melting meats and vegetables form a great base for a comforting feast. Slower cooking methods, braising for instance, come into their own here, and certain ingredients, such as silken tofu, provide this texture with little to no cooking involved.

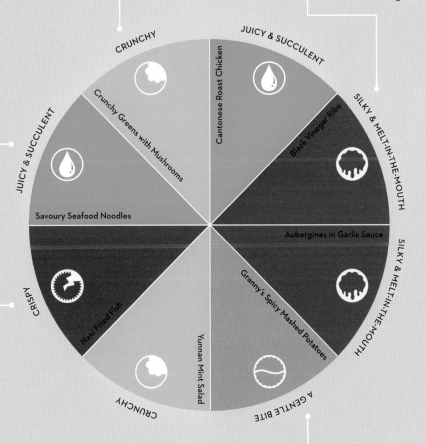

CRUNCHY

JUICY & SUCCULENT

SILKY & MELT-IN-THE-MOUTH

JUICY & SUCCULENT

SILKY & MELT-IN-THE-MOUTH

CRISPY

A GENTLE BITE

CRUNCHY

Cantonese Roast Chicken

Black Vinegar Ribs

Crunchy Greens with Mushrooms

Savoury Seafood Noodles

Aubergines in Garlic Sauce

Naxi Fried Fish

Granny's Spicy Mashed Potatoes

Yunnan Mint Salad

 Crispy: This workhorse texture often gets the starring role in a feast and is achieved through pan-frying, deep-frying or even baking, which create an immediate seal from scorching hot oil or high heat and crisped edges around the food.

 A Gentle Bite: This texture works with the natural structure of your ingredient, whether it's soft and gentle or a little firm, and is usually achieved by steaming or poaching to seal the food while maintaining its natural texture. Soft pastries and pancakes also contribute a gentle bite.

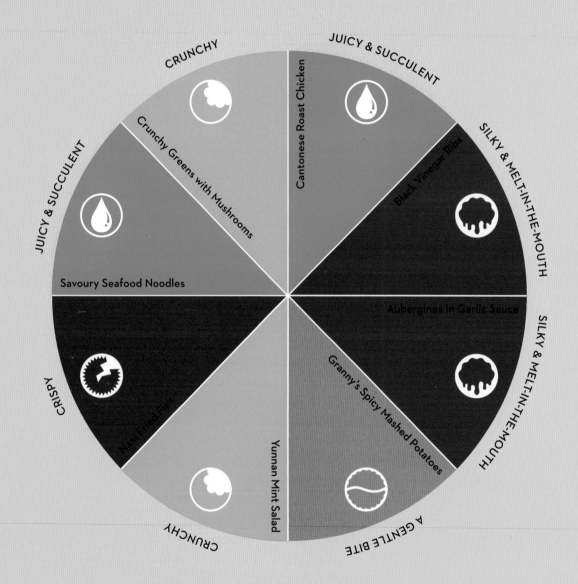

CRUNCHY

JUICY & SUCCULENT

SILKY & MELT-IN-THE-MOUTH

JUICY & SUCCULENT

Cantonese Roast Chicken

Crunchy Greens with Mushrooms

Black Vinegar Ribs

Savoury Seafood Noodles

Aubergines in Garlic Sauce

SILKY & MELT-IN-THE-MOUTH

CRISPY

Granny's Spicy Mashed Potatoes

Naxi Fried Fish

Yunnan Mint Salad

CRUNCHY

A GENTLE BITE

CHINESE

With my dad frequently working in China, I was lucky enough to experience the delights of real Chinese feasts and extravagant business banquets when I was growing up. In Chinese tradition, when it comes to sharing food there are certain rules of etiquette that you are taught to abide by. Over time, I began to enjoy them, their nuances and cultural specificity.

One of the first things I was taught is that if someone offers to buy you a meal, you absolutely must fight with them to pay the bill, then after a bit of a battle, you have to concede and let the banquet begin. Then, you must accept anything that is put in front of you, whether you like it or not. Even though I wanted to make a good impression on my dad's colleagues, this was a tough rule for me to follow, as a kid with a fairly Westernized palate. But this eating discipline widened my horizons to a world of food that I would have never encountered otherwise. The beauty of a Chinese banquet is that there is always a plethora of options available. So unless the host is unusually watchful, it's easy to pick what you want to eat without raising any attention if something is pushed aside in your own little rice bowl.

Ensuring every guest has equal access to the feast when laying the table is hard, and this is why traditional Chinese restaurants always have round tables. In fact, most big Chinese restaurants have an awesome trick up their sleeve where they can completely transform their seating plan within minutes by merely rolling a massive round tabletop over to a smaller table and plonking it on top, followed by a lazy Susan, in order to accommodate bigger groups and more food. Ideally, no one should ever be more than arm's reach from the next or best dish on the table. Chinese banqueting may be formal in one sense, but don't be fooled – there are no airs and graces once the food arrives, so just dig in!

Outside of Hong Kong, where the Cantonese fare was much closer to our family's home cooking, many of my first banqueting experiences in China took place in regions that are less well known internationally. My dad was one of the first overseas managers to pave the way for large Western pharmaceuticals opening up in Kunming, the capital of Yunnan province in southwest China, and damn do they know how to eat there! A significant proportion of Yunnan's population comes from some 25 ethnic minority communities, and this has a substantial impact on the food. So you'll notice a few more rustic dishes in my suggested banquet that come from this region of China, alongside some dishes with influences from Sichuan and, of course, Canton.

The showstopper dish for your Chinese home feast, Cantonese Roast Chicken, must be on the go a day in advance and left to marinate overnight, but once it's slow-roasting the next day you'll have plenty of time to prepare and cook your other chosen dishes. Both the Black Vinegar Ribs and the Aubergines in Garlic Sauce are perfect for cooking in advance, ready just to reheat before serving. Once the potatoes for Granny's Spicy Mashed Potatoes are steamed, get everything set up to finish off the stir-fry at the very last minute. When you've got a bit of time, prepare the mint for the Yunnan Mint Salad and have the leaves sitting in an airtight container in the fridge, with their dressing stored separately, ready to assemble just before bringing it to the table. To avoid trying to cook them at the same time and running out of hob space, I would then recommend choosing either the Naxi Fried Fish, serving it straight off the hot pan, or the Savoury Seafood Noodles. Towards the end of your feast preparations, get the stock on to blanch the greens for the Crunchy Greens with Mushrooms and then you're just one quick stir-fry away from sitting down for your feast.

CANTONESE ROAST CHICKEN

1.5kg (3lb 5oz) whole corn-fed
  chicken, spatchcocked
1 teaspoon baking powder
½ teaspoon salt
vegetable oil

MARINADE
½ thumb-sized piece of ginger,
  peeled and finely chopped
2 teaspoons Chinese five spice
1 teaspoon salt

GLAZE
1½ teaspoons salt
6 tablespoons honey
3 tablespoons rice vinegar
2 tablespoons light soy sauce

SPICED SALT
2 teaspoons Sichuan
  peppercorns
1 teaspoon salt
½ teaspoon sugar

It's a conundrum to recreate this Chinese restaurant classic at home, with limitations of space, as the chicken is usually hung out to dry, so equipment, hygiene concerns and paranoid family members need to be thought about. But I've found a reasonable way that my wife seems to tolerate. Although this is far simpler than the traditional methods, the process still takes a while. It's best to start early the day before you plan to serve.

1. Day 1: Place the spatchcocked chicken in a roasting tray that will fit in your fridge. Run your fingers between the skin and the meat to separate, while keeping the skin intact. Mix the marinade ingredients together, then rub it well around the cavity of the chicken only, trying not to get any on the skin.

2. Mix the glaze ingredients together, then brush a generous layer onto the skin. Cover the chicken with another tray – ideally perforated to allow air to circulate – or a sheet of foil pierced with a few holes. Place in the fridge for 2–3 hours. Then brush the skin again with the glaze and chill for another 2–3 hours. Brush once more with the glaze before leaving it in the fridge overnight.

3. For the spiced salt, toast the Sichuan peppercorns in a dry pan, swirling them around on a medium heat for 1–2 minutes until they pop and become fragrant. Then grind them using a pestle and mortar or spice grinder and mix with the salt and sugar.

4. Day 2: Remove the chicken from the fridge, lift off the tray or foil and rub the baking powder and salt all over the skin to dry out further. Leave the chicken to come up to room temperature for at least 1 hour, if not 2, dabbing any wet patches with kitchen paper every 30 minutes. If you are worried about leaving uncovered meat out, cover with a mesh food cover to prevent any intrusions!

5. Preheat the oven to 130°C/300°F/Gas Mark 2. Brush the chicken with a light coating of vegetable oil all over the skin, then place on a wire rack set over a roasting tray. Roast for 55 minutes. Increase the oven temperature to 180°C/400°F/Gas Mark 6 and roast for another 15 minutes to crisp the skin. Chop the chicken into pieces and serve with the spiced salt on the side.

C H I N E S E

BLACK VINEGAR RIBS

Sweet and sour is the go-to taste experience to punctuate the start, middle or end of any good Chinese feast. When you cook ribs like this, the layers of flavour will keep you coming back for more, alternating between mouthfuls of fluffy rice. The glaze on the outside of the meat creates a lovely chew, alongside a natural sweetness and lingering savouriness achieved by poaching the ribs first. The distinctive flavour of the silky sauce from the Chinkiang (black) vinegar makes a unique treat in itself.

1 thumb-sized piece of ginger, peeled and finely sliced

5–6 garlic cloves, roughly chopped

800g (1lb 12oz) pork spareribs, cut into 3–4cm (1¼–1½ inch) bite-sized pieces – ask your butcher to chop them for you

4–5 spring onions, roughly chopped, plus extra to garnish

vegetable oil

SAUCE

6 tablespoons Chinkiang vinegar (swapsies: rice vinegar)

4 tablespoons dark soy sauce

2 tablespoons Shaoxing rice wine (swapsies: dry sherry)

100g (3½oz) palm sugar (swapsies: soft brown sugar)

POACHING LIQUID

5 star anise

1 cinnamon stick

3 bay leaves

1 litre (1¾ pints) chicken stock

100ml (3½fl oz) Shaoxing rice wine (swapsies: dry sherry)

3 tablespoons light soy sauce

1. Mix the sauce ingredients together in a small saucepan or wok, bring to a boil on a medium heat and continue boiling for 5 minutes or so until all the sugar has dissolved.

2. **Build Your Wok Clock:** Start at 12 o'clock with half the ginger and garlic, followed by the poaching liquid ingredients, the pork ribs, then the rest of the ginger and garlic, all the spring onions and lastly the sauce.

3. Heat 1 tablespoon of vegetable oil in a large saucepan on a medium heat. Add the first batch of ginger and garlic and fry until they have started to brown around the edges. Then add the star anise, cinnamon and bay leaves and fry for 30 seconds. Pour in the rest of the poaching liquid ingredients and bring to a boil, then add the pork ribs, reduce the heat to low and simmer for 45 minutes.

4. Heat a wok or saucepan to medium heat. Add the rest of the ginger and garlic along with the spring onions and stir-fry for 1–2 minutes. Add the sauce and bring to a boil, then reduce the heat to medium-low.

5. Remove the ribs from the poaching liquid with a slotted spoon and place them directly in the bubbling sauce. Boil on a medium heat for 10–15 minutes, stirring them through once in a while, until the sauce has reduced by half and turned into a glaze around the ribs. Transfer to a platter, garnish with extra spring onion and serve.

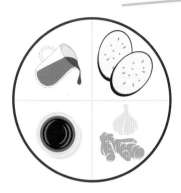

½ teaspoon salt
1 tablespoon cornflour
2 Chinese long aubergines
    (swapsies: 1 large aubergine),
    diagonally sliced into about
    4–5cm (1½–2 inch) lengths
½ thumb-sized piece of ginger,
    peeled and cut into
    matchsticks
4 garlic cloves, finely chopped
100ml (3½fl oz) vegetable stock
vegetable oil

SAUCE
2 tablespoons mushroom
    vegetarian stir-fry sauce
    (swapsies: oyster sauce)
1½ tablespoons Shaoxing rice
    wine (swapsies: dry sherry)
1 tablespoon light soy sauce
½ teaspoon sugar
dash of dark soy sauce

AUBERGINES IN GARLIC SAUCE

A great braise always starts with frying the ingredients before simmering them in a sauce. Much like cooking a steak, searing the aubergine here works to seal in the natural moisture of the 'meaty' vegetable, allowing it to then cook through in the sauce while keeping its silky, melt-in-the-mouth texture. Restaurants often initially deep-fry the aubergine, but I feel this is an unnecessary step for home cooking. If you're keen on less washing-up, just cook the whole dish in a frying pan.

1. Massage the salt and cornflour into the aubergine pieces.

2. Mix the sauce ingredients together in a small bowl.

3. **Build Your Wok Clock:** Start at 12 o'clock with the aubergine pieces, followed by the ginger and garlic, then the sauce and lastly the vegetable stock.

4. Heat 2 tablespoons of vegetable oil in a large frying pan or wok to a medium heat. Add the aubergine pieces, spacing them out in the pan and mopping up a little of the oil with each piece, then turn them over straight away so that they absorb as little oil as possible. Fry for about 4–5 minutes on each side until lightly charred – you may need to do this in batches to ensure every piece is browned well on both sides.

5. Push the aubergine aside to make enough space in the pan for the ginger and garlic, adding another ½ tablespoon of vegetable oil if needed, and stir-fry the ginger and garlic for 30 seconds. Fold together with the aubergine, returning any other batches to the pan. Stir-fry for 1–2 minutes.

6. Increase the heat to high, and once smoking hot, pour in the sauce, bring it to a vigorous boil and boil for 1–2 minutes to caramelize well. Then pour in the vegetable stock, reduce the heat to medium-low and simmer for 8–10 minutes to cook the aubergine through gently and allow the sauce to reduce to a smooth, glossy consistency.

SAVOURY SEAFOOD NOODLES

This dish works as a midweek meal, but you'll also find something similar at many a wedding banquet – incidentally one of the very few times a Chinese feast is served in courses.

1. Butterfly the prawns by running a knife down the backs through the meat to open them out, then rinse under cold running water to remove the black digestive cord. Dab the prawns and scallops dry with kitchen paper and place in a bowl.

2. Mix the sauce ingredients together in a small bowl.

3. **Build Your Wok Clock:** Start at 12 o'clock with the scallops, followed by the prawns, the soaked or fresh noodles and then the ginger, garlic, spring onions, asparagus and mangetout, the sauce and lastly the cornflour paste.

4. Bring a large frying pan to a high heat and add a small amount of vegetable oil, swirling it around the pan until it reaches smoking point. Add the scallops and prawns, press down on them gently with a spatula and sear for 30-60 seconds until brown around the edges. Turn over and repeat on the other side. Transfer to a clean bowl.

5. Add 1-2 tablespoons of vegetable oil to the pan, scatter in the noodles loosely and reduce the heat to medium-low. Press the noodles down into the pan firmly and fry for 4-5 minutes until they begin to crisp up and stick together slightly and turn golden on the underside. Flip the noodle nest over and repeat until crispy and golden on the other side. Carefully transfer the noodles to a large serving plate.

6. Heat 1 tablespoon of vegetable oil in a wok to a high heat. Add the ginger, garlic and spring onions and stir-fry for 30 seconds. Add the asparagus and stir-fry for 1 minute, then add the mangetout. Heat the wok to smoking point, pour in the sauce and bring to a vigorous boil. Add the scallops and prawns and continue to boil while folding the seafood through the vegetables for 30-60 seconds. Stir 3-4 teaspoons of the cornflour paste into the boiling sauce and cook until it starts to thicken slightly and you have a silky-smooth sauce. Pour over the crispy noodles and serve.

225g (8oz) dried egg noodles, soaked in hot water for 3 minutes until tender, then drained and dried for 10 minutes, or fresh fine egg noodles
8 raw peeled tiger prawns
12 scallops, cleaned and roes removed if buying whole
1 thumb-sized piece of ginger, peeled and cut into matchsticks
1 garlic clove, finely sliced
2 spring onions, roughly chopped
bunch of asparagus, trimmed and diagonally sliced into 4cm (1½ inch) lengths
100g (3½oz) mangetout, topped and tailed
2 teaspoons cornflour mixed with 2 teaspoons cold water
vegetable oil

SAUCE
125ml (4fl oz) chicken stock
2 tablespoons Shaoxing rice wine (swapsies: dry sherry)
1½ tablespoons oyster sauce
1 tablespoon light soy sauce
dash of sesame oil
pinch of white or black pepper
pinch of sugar

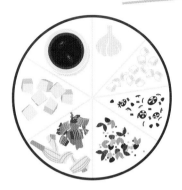

GRANNY'S SPICY MASHED POTATOES

This take on mashed potato will change your taste buds forever and make you realize that spicy carbs on carbs – it's usually served with rice and many other dishes – makes an unstoppable feasting combo. The dish was supposedly invented by an old grandma of Yunnan province in China, who may have been lacking some teeth but definitely hadn't lost her sense of taste and clearly knew how to cook.

2 large white potatoes
    (any variety), peeled and cut
    into 2cm (¾ inch) chunks
3–4 garlic cloves, finely chopped
3–4 spring onions, finely sliced
    into rings, white and green
    parts kept separate
1 large red chilli, finely chopped
handful of pickled mustard
    greens (za cai) (swapsies:
    Sichuan ya cai, sauerkraut,
    kimchi or a mixture of
    gherkins and capers),
    chopped
1 baby fennel bulb,
    roughly chopped
1–2 tablespoons Lao Gan Ma
    or Chiu Chow chilli oil
vegetable oil

DRY SPICES
½ teaspoon fennel seeds
½ teaspoon chilli powder
½ teaspoon Sichuan
    peppercorns, finely
    ground to a powder
½ teaspoon salt

1. Place the potatoes on a heatproof plate or tray to fit inside a bamboo steamer basket or your wok. Fill the wok about one-third up with boiling water and, if using, place the steamer with the plate or tray of potatoes in the wok and cover the steamer with its lid. If you don't have a steamer, place a heatproof bowl in the middle of the wok, protruding just above the water's surface, then place the plate or tray of potatoes on top and cover the wok with its domed lid. Keep the water on a gentle boil to steam the potatoes for 20 minutes until fork tender.

2. Mix the dry spices together in a small bowl.

3. **Build Your Wok Clock:** Start at 12 o'clock with the garlic, followed by the spring onion whites, red chilli, the dry spices, pickled vegetables, fennel and lastly the steamed potatoes and chilli oil.

4. Heat 1–2 tablespoons of vegetable oil in a wok to medium heat. Add the garlic and then continue working around the wok clock up until the pickled vegetables, adding each ingredient in turn and stir-frying for 10–15 seconds after each addition. Add the pickled vegetables and stir-fry for 30–60 seconds. Then add the fennel and stir-fry for 2 minutes. Lastly, add the steamed potatoes and start to mash them while continuously folding the spices into the potatoes as you go. Stir-fry and fold the potatoes together for 1–2 minutes until mashed and well mixed. Garnish with the spring onion greens and then pour over the chilli oil to serve.

YUNNAN MINT SALAD

large bunch of mint
2–3 ice cubes

DRESSING
1 garlic clove, finely chopped
1 birds' eye chilli, finely chopped
1 teaspoon sugar
¼ teaspoon salt
2 tablespoons Chinkiang
   vinegar (swapsies: rice
   vinegar)
juice of ½ lime
½ teaspoon Chiu Chow chili oil
½ teaspoon sesame oil

You will notice that a few Yunnan dishes have found their way into this suggested feast. As kids, we quite often followed my dad around China on his various business travels, and Yunnan province, located in the southwest of China, was a region of fond feasting memories. Yunnan's plethora of ethnic minorities, a unique feature of the region, and its proximity to South East Asia have an enormous influence on its flavours and ingredients, which you don't often find in the central or eastern parts of China. This mint salad is a perfect balancing act of flavour, texture and colour all in one dish to create an unusually fresh and crunchy side, with black vinegar making another appearance to help tie the whole feast together.

1. Pick the mint leaves, then wash and place them in cold water with the ice cubes to crisp up. Drain just before serving.

2. Mix the dressing ingredients together in a small bowl, then pour the dressing over the mint leaves when ready to serve.

NAXI FRIED FISH

Lijiang in the northwest of Yunnan province and home to many Naxi people has become a popular tourist town for its old rooftops and cobbled streets filled with a maze of footbridges crossing streams and canals. Its walkways are lined with terraced restaurants, tea houses and boutiques. International influence is aplenty, but there are many traditional diners that serve earthy home-cooked food like this fish dish.

300–400g (10½–14oz) whole trout (swapsies: bream, carp or sea bream), cleaned, gutted and descaled
6–8 tablespoons cornflour, seasoned with a pinch of salt and black pepper
2 tablespoons preserved fermented black beans, soaked in hot water for 10 minutes, then drained
½–1 tablespoon chilli flakes, to taste
handful of blanched unsalted peanuts
½ thumb-sized piece of ginger, peeled and cut into matchsticks
½ onion, finely sliced
3 spring onions, cut into matchsticks
2 long green chillies, roughly chopped
vegetable oil

SAUCE
2 tablespoons light soy sauce
2 tablespoons water
1 tablespoon chilli bean sauce
1 tablespoon oyster sauce
½ tablespoon dark soy sauce
1 teaspoon sugar

1. Make 2–3 diagonal slits across the skin of the fish on each side. Then coat the entire fish with the seasoned cornflour, making sure that the fins and tail are well dusted so that they get nice and crispy, adding more cornflour if required until the fish is dry to the touch. Lift the fish up and give it a little tap on both sides to dust off any excess cornflour. Set aside on a plate.

2. Mix the sauce ingredients together in a small bowl.

3. **Build Your Wok Clock:** Start at 12 o'clock with the fish, then the black beans, followed by the chilli flakes, peanuts, ginger, onion, spring onions, green chillies and lastly the sauce.

4. Heat 2–3 tablespoons of vegetable oil in a large frying pan to a high heat. Place the whole fish in the pan and fry for 1 minute, pressing down on the fins with a spatula to crisp them. Reduce the heat to medium-low and fry for 4–5 minutes, pressing down to sear well. Turn over and repeat on the other side until crispy.

5. Meanwhile, heat 2 tablespoons of vegetable oil in a wok to a medium heat, add the black beans and stir-fry for a minute or so. Reduce the heat to low, add the chilli flakes and stir-fry for 1–2 minutes. Then add the peanuts and stir-fry for 2 minutes to brown the nuts and release their oil. Increase the heat to high, and once smoking hot, add the ginger, onion, spring onions and chillies in turn, stir-frying for 30 seconds after each addition. Pour in the sauce and bring to a boil, then continue to cook and stir on a high heat until it has reduced and thickened to a light syrupy texture. Remove from the heat.

6. Once the fish is crispy on both sides, transfer to a serving plate. Reheat the sauce if necessary, pour over the fish and serve immediately.

6 dried shiitake mushrooms,
    soaked in hot water for at
    least 1 hour or boiled for
    20 minutes, then drained
300g (10½oz) Chinese broccoli
    (*kai lan*), Tenderstem broccoli
    or any other leafy greens,
    cut into 4–5cm (1½–2 inch)
    lengths
8 garlic cloves, finely sliced
vegetable oil
salt and pepper

STOCK
300ml (10fl oz) vegetable stock
1 tablespoon light soy sauce
1 tablespoon oyster sauce
    (swapsies: vegetarian
    stir-fry sauce)

CRUNCHY GREENS WITH MUSHROOMS

I love all types of stalky deep-green vegetables, and while this dish is often prepared using Chinese broccoli (*kai lan*), it's interchangeable with Tenderstem broccoli, kale, cavolo nero or even the leaves of a cauliflower that might otherwise be thrown away. The classic way to cook this is just with garlic, but I love the texture of crispy dried shiitake mushrooms, as they add a rich savoury flavour to the slightly bittersweet leaves.

1. Squeeze any excess water out of the soaked mushrooms and then press firmly with kitchen paper to dry them before finely slicing them.

2. Mix the stock ingredients together in a jug.

3. **Build Your Wok Clock:** Start at 12 o'clock with the stock, followed by the greens, shiitake mushrooms and then the garlic.

4. Bring the stock to a vigorous boil in a wok, add the greens and boil for 3–4 minutes. Strain through a sieve set over a mixing bowl to reserve the stock.

5. Return the wok to a medium heat to dry, then add 2 tablespoons of vegetable oil followed by the mushrooms and stir-fry for 2–3 minutes until they begin to crisp up around the edges. Add the garlic and stir-fry on a medium heat for 1–2 minutes until it starts to turn golden brown but not burn. Season with a pinch of salt and pepper and then remove from the heat.

6. Place the greens on a serving plate, pour over a ladleful of the hot stock and top with the crispy mushrooms and garlic.

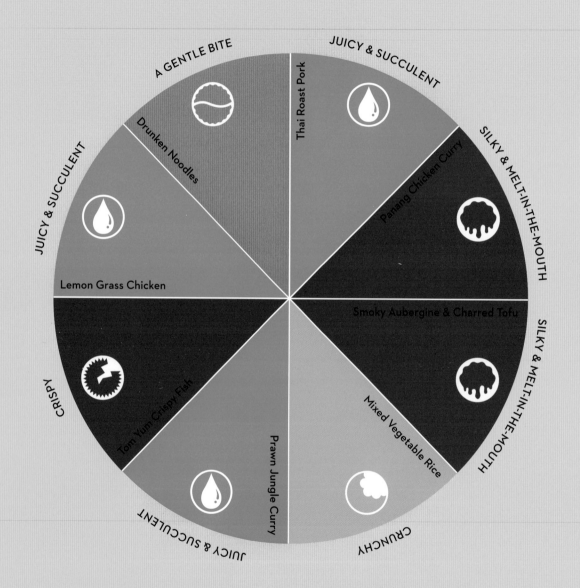

A GENTLE BITE

JUICY & SUCCULENT

Thai Roast Pork

SILKY & MELT-IN-THE-MOUTH

Panang Chicken Curry

Drunken Noodles

JUICY & SUCCULENT

Lemon Grass Chicken

Smoky Aubergine & Charred Tofu

SILKY & MELT-IN-THE-MOUTH

CRISPY

Tom Yum Crispy Fish

Mixed Vegetable Rice

Prawn Jungle Curry

JUICY & SUCCULENT

CRUNCHY

THAI

No matter where I'm travelling, the first place I usually head for, soon after landing in a new country, is a local market or supermarket. I think it's by far the best way to get a glimpse into what might be good to eat or order at the local restaurants. If you can see what's fresh in the markets, wherever you are, not only will you begin to understand what ingredients might be best to cook or eat, you'll also glean some insight into the prominent flavours of that area.

The last time I was in Bangkok, for example, all the fishmonger stands in the markets were full of river prawns that looked like cousins of the Scottish langoustine. Low and behold, I ended up seeing the same kind of prawns being cooked in most of the restaurants visited during the same trip. There were also varying types of aubergine, from teeny tiny pea aubergines to gigantic purple aubergines that looked more like baby seals than vegetables. While guidebooks are a great place to start your research before visiting somewhere new, they can only take you so far.

The beauty of any Thai fresh food market is that, dotted in between the fresh fruit and vegetable stands, there are often little snack stops, a much-welcome sight if you're perpetually hungry like me, or if you just fancy a bite to eat or a hit of something sweet. Keep your eyes peeled for these hidden treasures selling freshly made sticky mango rice (see page 199) with hand-squeezed coconut milk, sweet–savoury coconut pancakes (kanom krok) or cups of lime juice squeezed to order to cool you down as you shop.

When I first started School of Wok, we offered an intensive feasting cookery course in which, over ten weeks, I would teach people not just how to cook individual dishes but also how and where to shop for ingredients and how to plan an Asian meal. During the last lesson, we would plan the menu and go to the market together to shop before cooking up a feast for numerous guests. The concept came from Thailand, where all the cookery classes and market tours I've ever taken brought you back to the basics of food by reminding you that shopping in local markets in search of the freshest produce is the first stage of feasting – feasting with your eyes – resulting in a homely, comforting feasting experience for all those involved.

So if you decide to cook up a Thai feast, or any of the feasts in this book for that matter, I highly recommend that you first take a trip to an Asian supermarket, if available locally, or even a local butcher's shop and fishmonger rather than a big brand supermarket to wander about a bit. Let your eyes start the feast early to truly enjoy the whole process.

When preparing your feast, the Thai Roast Pork needs to marinate overnight in the fridge, and the Panang Chicken Curry can be made a day in advance too. Then everything for the Smoky Aubergine & Charred Tofu can be prepared beforehand, ready to assemble just before you cook up any other dishes, and the vegetables for the Mixed Vegetable Rice can be chopped and prepped while the rice is cooking. You can then get on with the sauce for the Prawn Jungle Curry before popping in the prepared prawns a bit later. As should always be the case, finish cooking with one or more of the fried dishes – Tom Yum Crispy Fish, Lemon Grass Chicken or Drunken Noodles – so that they can be served piping hot straight from the wok.

PANANG CHICKEN CURRY

Panang, meaning 'crossed', is easily mispronounced – the word should sound more like 'pah naing'. Its origins began along the Cambodian–Thai border and was named in reference to the crossing of the bird's legs, to lock in the spice paste flavours. I've gone for whole leg joints to keep the recipe simple, yet succulent while showcasing the silky smooth curry sauce.

4 whole chicken legs
3 lime leaves
300ml (10fl oz) coconut milk
100ml (3½fl oz) chicken stock
2 white potatoes, peeled and
  cut into large chunks
2–3 tablespoons fish sauce
1 tablespoon palm sugar
  (swapsies: soft brown sugar)
vegetable oil
1 large red chilli, finely sliced,
  to garnish

CURRY PASTE
2 teaspoons coriander seeds
1 teaspoon cumin seeds
½ teaspoon black peppercorns
10–15 dried red chillies, soaked
  in hot water for 10–15 minutes,
  then drained and finely
  chopped
4–5 Thai shallots (swapsies:
  1 brown shallot), finely chopped
2 garlic cloves, finely chopped
2 lime leaves, finely chopped
1 lemon grass stalk, trimmed,
  bruised and finely chopped
½ thumb-sized piece of ginger
  or galangal, peeled and
  finely chopped
handful of coriander roots
  or stalks, finely chopped
1 tablespoon ready-made
  crispy fried onions or
  shallots (optional)

1. For the curry paste, toast the coriander and cumin seeds and black peppercorns together in a dry pan on a medium heat for 1–2 minutes until fragrant. Then pound with the rest of the curry paste ingredients using a pestle and mortar, adding them one at a time, or blitz in a food processor to form a smooth paste (you may need to add a tablespoon or so of water if using a machine).

2. Massage the chicken with 2–3 tablespoons of the curry paste, keeping the rest of the paste aside to make the curry sauce.

3. **Build your wok clock:** Start at 12 o'clock with the chicken legs, followed by the rest of the paste, the lime leaves, coconut milk, chicken stock, potatoes, fish sauce and lastly the sugar.

4. Heat 1–2 tablespoons of vegetable oil in a frying pan to a medium-high heat and pan fry the chicken pieces for 5–6 minutes on each side until golden brown.

5. Meanwhile, heat 1–2 tablespoons of vegetable oil in a thick based wok or saucepan on a low heat, add the remaining curry paste and lime leaves and cook through while stirring for 4–5 minutes until fragrant and deep red. Now, pour in 75ml (2½fl oz) of the coconut milk, stir and then allow to boil, before adding the next 75ml (2½fl oz). Return to a boil and then add the remaining coconut milk and the chicken stock and bring to boil once more. Add the potatoes and the seared chicken pieces into the curry sauce and turn the heat down to low and allow to simmer for 30–35 minutes. Ten minutes before serving, turn the heat up and bring to a vigorous boil and continue to cook until the sauce has reduced to a double cream consistency.

6. Lastly, season with the fish sauce and palm sugar, allow the palm sugar to melt into the curry sauce and then taste, adjust the seasoning if necessary and serve. Garnish with sliced red chilli.

T
H
A
I

THAI ROAST PORK

1kg (2lb 4oz) boneless pork neck
   or shoulder

MARINADE
2 tablespoons oyster sauce
1 tablespoon light soy sauce
1 tablespoon dark soy sauce
1 tablespoon fish sauce
½ tablespoon palm sugar
   (swapsies: soft brown sugar)
1 tablespoon water

DIPPING SAUCE
1 tablespoon dry rice grains
1 teaspoon chilli powder
3 Thai shallots (swapsies:
   ½ red onion), finely sliced
1 spring onion, finely chopped
small handful of coriander,
   leaves picked and
   finely chopped
4 tablespoons fish sauce
2 tablespoons palm sugar
   (swapsies: soft brown sugar)
juice of 1 lime

Popular all over the world, this Thai pork dish, *kor moo yang*, is so simple to make at home. I remember eating it for the first time in Hong Kong, where there were numerous Thai restaurants near Sai Kung to the east of Kowloon. My memories of the dish may not be true to its authentic form, but they are borne out of the powerful impact that sharing a Thai feast with my sisters and parents had on our whole family. The perfectly sweet and salty char on the roast meat will prompt you to question whether you have made enough, no matter how much you make, so try to add a few other dishes to fight over too!

1. Mix the marinade ingredients together, then massage the marinade into the pork. Place the pork in a sealable food bag or on a tightly covered tray and refrigerate overnight.

2. For the dipping sauce, toast the rice grains in a dry wok on a medium heat for 4-5 minutes until uniformly golden brown. Add the chilli powder and mix well. Allow to cool, then grind the spiced grains to a powder using a pestle and mortar or spice grinder.

3. Mix the rest of the dipping sauce ingredients with the spiced rice powder in a ramekin or small bowl.

4. Preheat the oven to 150°C/340°F/Gas Mark 3½. Place the pork in a roasting tray and roast for 1 hour.

5. Change the oven function to grill and preheat it to 230°C/450°F. Grill the pork for 5-6 minutes until charred on one side, then flip it over and baste with any excess marinade. Grill the other side for another 5-6 minutes until charred. Remove the pork from the oven, cut it into thin slices and serve with the dipping sauce on the side.

T
H
A
I

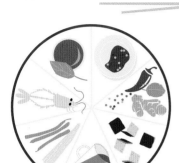

PRAWN JUNGLE CURRY

The deep red colour of this dish, from the vibrant forests of Northern Thailand, says it all – there is no coconut water or milk here to mellow out the spice. It's mountainous, earthy and driven by the fragrance of the lime leaves, the spices and the simplicity of the cooking process. Other types of seafood, fish and chicken will all work here, or you can choose pork, beef or lamb, just increase the cooking time significantly to produce the best results. The flavour profile of the dish should be salty and spicy rather than sweet. If you can find lesser ginger to use instead of regular, you will get an even earthier forest flavour. Or try adding bamboo shoots or shrimp paste too.

8–10 peeled large tiger prawns
½ thumb-sized piece of ginger, peeled and cut into matchsticks
6 lime leaves
a string (or 1 teaspoon) black or green peppercorns
2 green chillies, pierced
3–4 Thai aubergines, quartered (swapsies: 1 small aubergine, cut into chunks)
500ml (18fl oz) chicken stock
handful of green beans, cut into 3–4cm (1¼–1½ inch) lengths
6 baby sweetcorn, sliced
2–3 tablespoons fish sauce
handful of holy basil leaves (swapsies: Thai sweet basil)
vegetable oil

CURRY PASTE
10 dried red chillies, soaked, drained and finely chopped
2 Thai shallots (swapsies: ½ red onion), finely chopped
4 garlic cloves, finely chopped
3 red chillies, finely chopped
2 birds' eye chillies, finely chopped
1 thumb-sized piece ginger, peeled and finely chopped
2 lemon grass stalks, trimmed, bruised and finely chopped
small handful of coriander stalks, finely chopped
4 lime leaves

1. Pound the curry paste ingredients together using a pestle and mortar, adding them one at a time, or blitz them in a food processor to form a smooth paste (you may need to add a tablespoon or so of water if using a machine).

2. Butterfly the prawns by running a knife down the backs through the meat to open them out, then rinse under cold running water to remove the black digestive cord.

3. **Build Your Wok Clock:** Start at 12 o'clock with 3–4 tablespoons of the curry paste (freeze the rest in ice-cube trays for later use), followed by the ginger, lime leaves, green peppercorns, green chillies, aubergines, chicken stock, green beans, baby sweetcorn, prawns and lastly the fish sauce and holy basil.

4. Heat 1–2 tablespoons of vegetable oil in a thick-based wok or saucepan to a medium heat. Add the curry paste, stir well and cook through for 3–4 minutes until fragrant and deeper red in colour. Add the ginger, lime leaves, green peppercorns and green chillies together and stir-fry for 1–2 minutes. Then add the aubergines and stir-fry for 4–5 minutes. Pour in the chicken stock and bring to a boil, then reduce the heat to medium-low and simmer for 15 minutes. Stir in the green beans and baby sweetcorn followed by the prawns. Increase the heat to medium and continue to simmer for 3–4 minutes until the prawns have turned coral pink in colour. Season to taste with the fish sauce, then scatter the holy basil over the top to wilt into the curry while serving. Serve immediately.

handful of ready-fried tofu
(*tofu pok*)
2 long Thai aubergines
(swapsies: 1 large aubergine)
vegetable oil

MARINADE
1 tablespoon light soy sauce
1 teaspoon vegetable oil

DRESSING
½ teaspoon chilli powder
4–5 Thai shallots (swapsies:
½ red onion), finely sliced
2 spring onions, finely sliced
1 red chilli, finely sliced
handful of mint leaves,
finely chopped
1 tablespoon palm sugar
(swapsies: soft brown sugar)
2 tablespoons vegetarian fish
sauce (swapsies: light soy
sauce or fish sauce)
juice of ½ lime

SMOKY AUBERGINE & CHARRED TOFU

I find it incredible how smoked aubergine is incorporated into so many cuisines around the world. There's something extremely satisfying about the melt-in-the-mouth, silky texture you get from a well-charred aubergine. The skin essentially works to protect the flesh, allowing it to steam in its own juices. This soft and slippery texture is usually counterbalanced by freshly blanched or grilled prawns, but with a prawn curry already in our feast in this chapter, keeping this dish meat-free provides the necessary balance, and the texture of the tofu makes a fantastic alternative.

1. Preheat the oven to 210°C/450°F/Gas Mark 8.

2. Slice the fried tofu in half diagonally, creating little pyramid-shaped pieces and rub with the marinade ingredients.

3. For the dressing, lightly toast the chilli powder in a dry frying pan on a low heat for 30 seconds, then mix with the rest of the dressing ingredients in a small bowl.

4. Rub ½ tablespoon of vegetable oil all over the aubergines, place them in a roasting tray and roast for 30–35 minutes.

5. Meanwhile, heat a frying pan or griddle pan to a high heat, add the tofu cut side down and sear for about 3 minutes until charred. Remove from the pan and allow to cool.

6. Once the aubergines are cooked through, they will look and feel soft with the skin slightly wrinkled and you will be able to push a fork or knife straight through without any resistance. If there is still some resistance, return them to the oven for another 5 minutes and check again. Remove from the oven and allow to cool slightly, then peel and slice into 2–3cm (¾–1¼ inch) thick lengths. Arrange the aubergine pieces on a serving plate and top with the tofu, then pour the dressing over to serve. This dish can be served hot or at room temperature, but either way, it's best to pour the dressing over 5 minutes before serving to allow it to soak into the tofu and aubergine.

TOM YUM CRISPY FISH

This showstopper is the epitome of flavour, texture and colour balance, encapsulating the vibrancy of Thai cuisine. The fish is crispy but succulent, submerged in a puckeringly tart broth, with undertones of sweetness and a punch of savoury, salty and spicy flavours. This dish is unapologetically 'extra', memorable and worth the effort every time.

250g (9oz) whole sea bream
    (swapsies: sea bass, flounder
    or plaice), cleaned, gutted
    and descaled
100g (3½oz) cornflour,
    seasoned with 1 teaspoon
    salt and ½ teaspoon
    black pepper
5 lime leaves
200ml (7fl oz) chicken stock
1–2 tablespoons fish sauce
juice of 1 lime
vegetable oil

SPICE PASTE
10 dried red chillies,
    soaked in hot water for
    10–15 minutes, then drained
    and finely chopped
2 birds' eye chillies,
    finely chopped
2 garlic cloves, finely chopped
2 lemon grass stalks, trimmed,
    bruised and finely chopped
1 thumb-sized piece of ginger,
    peeled and finely chopped
handful of coriander stalks,
    finely chopped
2 tablespoons tamarind
    concentrate
½ tablespoon brown sugar
½ teaspoon salt

1. Make 5–6 diagonal slits across the skin of the whole fish on each side. Then coat the entire fish in the seasoned cornflour, making sure that the fins and tail are well dusted so that they get nice and crispy, adding more cornflour if required until the fish is dry to the touch. Then lift the fish up and give it a little tap on both sides to dust off any excess cornflour. Set aside on a plate.

2. Pound the spice paste ingredients together using a pestle and mortar, adding them one at a time, or blitz them in a food processor to form a smooth paste (you may need a tablespoon of water).

3. **Build Your Wok Clock:** Start at 12 o'clock with the lime leaves, followed by the spice paste, then the chicken stock, the fish, fish sauce and lastly the lime juice.

4. Heat 1–2 tablespoons of oil on a medium heat in a saucepan, add the lime leaves and spice paste and fry for 4–5 minutes until fragrant. Pour in the stock, stir and bring to a boil, then reduce to medium-low and simmer for 15 minutes to reduce by half.

5. Meanwhile, fill a wok one-third with oil and bring to a medium-high heat. Test the temperature by placing the tip of a wooden chopstick in the oil. If it starts to fizz after a second, the oil has reached the desired temperature. Carefully lay the fish in the hot oil and deep-fry for 2 minutes. Reduce the heat to medium and continue to fry for another 8–10 minutes, depending on the fish size. If you can see the bones peeking out where you have scored the fish, it is cooked through. Gently remove the fish from the oil with a slotted spoon or bamboo strainer and place on 2–3 sheets of kitchen paper to drain the excess oil for a minute or so.

6. Transfer the fish to a serving plate. Season the spicy broth with the fish sauce and lime juice, pour over the fish and serve immediately.

390g (13¾oz) jasmine rice
3 tablespoons desiccated
    coconut
1 green mango (swapsies:
    Granny Smith apple), peeled,
    stoned and in matchsticks
1 carrot, cut into matchsticks
handful of green beans,
    finely chopped
¼ red cabbage, finely shredded
100g (3½oz) beansprouts
2 lemon grass stalks, outer
    leaves peeled and reserved,
    inner parts finely chopped
5–6 lime leaves, finely shredded
½ pomelo, peeled, segmented
    and roughly chopped
390ml (13f oz) water

SPICE PASTE

lemon grass outer leaves
    (see above), finely chopped
3 Thai shallots (swapsies:
    ½ red onion), finely chopped
2 garlic cloves, finely chopped
2 lime leaves, finely chopped

SAUCE

1 tablespoon palm sugar
    (swapsies: soft brown sugar)
2 tablespoons each of tamarind
    concentrate and vegetarian
    fish sauce
3 tablespoons kecap manis
    (sweet soy sauce)

MIXED VEGETABLE RICE

The Thai name for this dish, *khao yum*, literally translates
as 'mixed rice' and is a Southern Thailand invention created
for its nutritional value. It's the perfect accompaniment to
any Thai meal with all the texture you need to balance out
the heaty feeling from melt-in-the-mouth meats and crispy
fried foods.

1. Pound the spice paste ingredients together using a pestle
and mortar, adding them one at a time, or blitz them in a food
processor to form a smooth paste (you may need a little water).

2. Mix the sauce ingredients together with 200ml (7fl oz) water.

3. Wash the rice under cold water at least 3 times, until the
water runs clear. Sieve and set aside.

4. Toast the desiccated coconut in a dry frying pan on a medium
heat for 4–5 minutes, stirring or tossing, until fragrant and
uniformly golden brown.

5. **Build Your Wok Clock:** Start at 12 o'clock with the rice,
followed by the paste, the sauce and lastly the prepared mango
and vegetables, the herbs, pomelo and toasted coconut.

6. Place the rice in a saucepan with the measured water. Cover
with a tight-fitting lid, place on a medium-high heat and bring
to a vigorous boil. Then reduce the heat to low and simmer with
the lid on for 12–15 minutes until the liquid has evaporated to the
point where you start to see air pockets form between some
of the rice grains. Replace the lid, turn the heat off and leave
the rice to sit for another 15 minutes.

7. Once the rice is cooking, place the paste in a saucepan, add
2 tablespoons water and bring to a boil on a medium heat and
cook for 3–4 minutes. Pour in the sauce and bring to a vigorous
boil, then reduce the heat to low and simmer for 5 minutes.
Turn the heat off.

8. Place the mango and all the vegetables, herbs, pomelo and
toasted coconut around a heap of rice, and serve the sauce
on the side ready to pour over the rice and mix well.

T
H
A
I

42

LEMON GRASS CHICKEN

I know with absolute certainty why this dish is a big hitter on the School of Wok YouTube channel. Like many Thai curries and stews, it's bold in flavour, but it can be cooked in a fraction of the time it takes for some of the slower-cooked recipes. That means less time spent salivating over the stove and more time to eat. This fierce stir-fry will make your mouth water and your guests' too – if you haven't picked it all out of the wok before they arrive!

4 skinless, boneless chicken
 thighs, cut into large chunks
1 tablespoon chicken stock
 or water
½ white or brown onion,
 finely sliced
2–3 lime leaves
handful of Thai basil leaves
vegetable oil

CURRY PASTE

3 spring onions, finely chopped
3 garlic cloves, finely chopped
2 lemon grass stalks, trimmed,
 bruised and finely chopped
½ thumb-sized piece of ginger,
 peeled and finely chopped
½ thumb-sized piece of
 turmeric, peeled and
 finely chopped (swapsies:
 1 teaspoon ground turmeric)
5–6 lime leaves, finely chopped
½ teaspoon salt

SAUCE

1 tablespoon light soy sauce
1 tablespoon fish sauce
½ tablespoon palm sugar
50ml (2fl oz) chicken stock

1. Pound the paste ingredients together using a pestle and mortar, adding them one at a time, or blitz them in a food processor to form a smooth paste (you may need to add a tablespoon or so of water).

2. Mix the sauce ingredients together in a small bowl.

3. Place the chicken pieces in a bowl. Mix 1 tablespoon of the curry paste with the chicken stock or water and massage it into the chicken.

4. **Build Your Wok Clock:** Start at 12 o'clock with the marinated chicken, followed by the rest of the curry paste, the onion, the sauce, lime leaves and lastly the Thai basil leaves.

5. Heat 1–2 tablespoons of vegetable oil in a wok on a high heat until smoking hot. Add the marinated chicken and sear for a minute without moving, then fold the chicken over to sear on the other side for another minute or so. Once the chicken has a nice crisp edge and is fully browned, push it to the side of the wok. Add the curry paste to the centre of the wok, then the onion and fold the chicken over the mixture to incorporate and prevent the meat from burning. After about a minute, the onion should start to wilt. At this point, increase the heat and allow the wok to smoke before pouring the sauce around the edges of the wok. Bring to a vigorous boil, fold the chicken through and stir-fry for 1–2 minutes. Add the lime leaves and Thai basil leaves to finish and serve immediately.

DRUNKEN NOODLES

Beer munchies at their best, these noodles were invented by a drunk chef who just needed something super-tasty to satisfy his hunger pangs. No matter whether you've had a few or not, these are a great treat and are absolutely fit for a feast.

1. Soak the noodles in hot water for 8–10 minutes until tender, then drain and leave to dry on a clean tea towel for 10 minutes.

2. Mix the sauce ingredients together in a small bowl.

3. **Build Your Wok Clock:** Start at 12 o'clock with the spring onions and red onion, followed by the garlic, chillies, broccoli, chicken, noodles, Thai basil leaves and lastly the sauce.

4. Heat 1 tablespoon of vegetable oil in a wok on a high heat until smoking hot. Add the spring onions and red onion and stir-fry for 30 seconds until the onions are lightly browned and softened. Reduce the heat to medium so as not to burn the onions and push them to the side of the wok. Add ½ tablespoon of vegetable oil to the centre of the wok, then add the garlic, chillies and broccoli in turn, stir-frying for 15–20 seconds after each addition, folding through to combine. Push the vegetables to the side of the wok. Add 1 tablespoon of vegetable oil to the centre of the wok and heat to smoking point. Add the chicken and sear for a minute or so, folding the vegetables over the top of the chicken. Then fold all the ingredients together and stir-fry for another minute. Add the noodles and stir-fry for a minute. Allow the wok to build up heat without stirring or folding for 30 seconds or so and then scatter the Thai basil leaves all over the stir-fry before pouring the sauce over all the ingredients. Stir-fry until the ingredients are thoroughly combined and all the sauce has been absorbed by the noodles, then serve immediately.

300g (10½oz) wide rice noodles
2 spring onions, roughly chopped
1 red onion, finely sliced
3 garlic cloves, finely sliced
2 birds' eye chillies, finely chopped
bunch of Chinese broccoli (*kai lan*) (swapsies: Tenderstem broccoli), sliced into 4-5cm (1½-2 inch) lengths
2 skinless, boneless chicken thighs, finely sliced
bunch of Thai basil, leaves picked
vegetable oil

SAUCE
2 tablespoons oyster sauce
1½ tablespoons fish sauce
1 tablespoon light soy sauce
1 tablespoon dark soy sauce
1 tablespoon chicken stock or water
2 teaspoons sugar

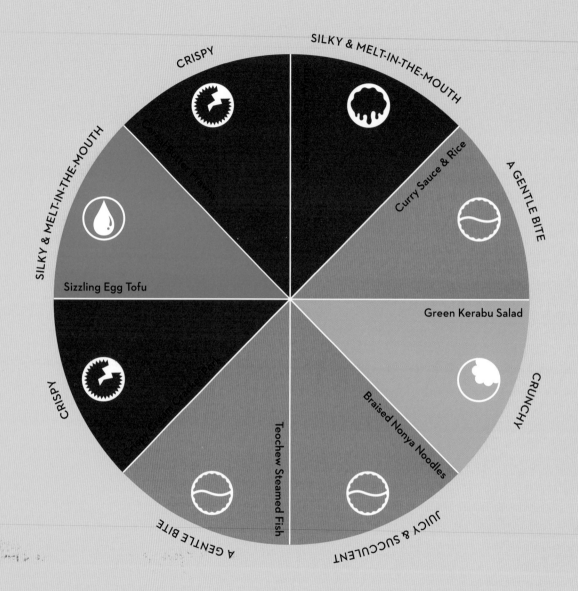

CRISPY

SILKY & MELT-IN-THE-MOUTH

SILKY & MELT-IN-THE-MOUTH

A GENTLE BITE

Curry Sauce & Rice

Caramelised Prawns

Sizzling Egg Tofu

Green Kerabu Salad

CRISPY

CRUNCHY

Crispy Cream Cracker Pork

Braised Nonya Noodles

A GENTLE BITE

Teochew Steamed Fish

JUICY & SUCCULENT

SINGAPOREAN

On landing in Singapore, the pristine environment, beautiful skyline and vertical gardens make a bold first impression, but its legendary hawker centres really bring it to life, and in December 2020, hawker culture was added to UNESCO's Representative List of Intangible Cultural Heritage of Humanity. Each and every stall in these massive, and often open-air, food courts specializes in one particular type of dish, cooking it over and over again. In this way, the recipes for these dishes, and the skills involved, are perfected over generations, becoming family legacies. So in Singapore, as well as in Malaysia, you could easily find yourself hawker-centre hopping and discovering the best of the best local food in every corner of this tiny city-state.

When Cher Loh, our senior chef tutor at School of Wok, and I reminisce about Singapore, satay naturally comes up in conversation. 'In Singapore, no one ever makes their own satay because it's just so good on the streets!' he reports. And it's true. You can buy satay at the local hawker centres or markets, pre-marinated and threaded onto sticks ready for you to simply plonk on the barbecue or in a pan at home. In fact, there's a whole street, slap bang in the middle of Singapore's central business district, dubbed Satay Street by the locals that every evening is buzzing with satay grills and satay sauce aplenty. All this talk of satay and I haven't actually included a recipe for it in this book(!), but there is a wok-fried satay recipe that's worth a try in my previous School of Wok book, *Delicious Asian Food in Minutes*. If you're a stickler for more traditional cooking, just thread the marinated meat onto some sticks and barbecue them for good measure.

Asked for other dishes he would add to his ideal feast, Cher puts rendang at the top, highlighting its oft-debated popularity as a dish 'claimed' by many Asian countries. But luckily for me, Cher's ancestral lineage is Indonesian, so he's OK with rendang finding its way into another chapter (see page 114)! Also at the top of his list is cereal butter prawns, alongside more rustic, home-style dishes like *Nonya chap chye*, which is an indication of how important neighbouring influences are when it comes to food, as he explains that *chap chye* would have originally come from Korean immigrants. And this underlines the variety of cultures that make up Singaporean cuisine. You'll find my version of *Nonya chap chye* here (see page 58), along with a recipe for Cereal Butter Prawns (see page 57). But overall, this chapter is driven by a hawker-centre classic 'buffet' of food known locally as 'scissors-cut rice' – see my Curry Sauce & Rice (page 54) – which works to bring some of these dishes together for an unforgettable feast.

To start your feast preparations, braising the Star Anise Soy Wings takes just minutes, and they will sit perfectly well ready to be reheated later. Then it's always wise to get your Curry Sauce & Rice cooking early on too – rice is one of those things you can't rush (I'd also strongly recommend using a rice cooker, which will save on hob space and keep your rice warm) – and the sauce can be reheated at the end. Then the Green Kerabu Salad can be prepped, and the Braised Nonya Noodles cooked, to be served warmed or at room temperature or reheated. Prepare the components of the Teochew Steamed Fish ahead ready to steam for 10 minutes before serving, then move on to the Wok Clocks for your choice of Crispy Cream Cracker Pork, Sizzling Egg Tofu or Cereal Butter Prawns, cooking in that order. Remember, it's perfectly OK to sit your guests down and bring a few freshly cooked dishes to the table soon after. While you don't want to hang around the kitchen all night and miss the food and fun, finishing the last-minute cooking and joining your guests a little while later is just fine.

CURRY SAUCE & RICE

There's a meal in Singapore called 'scissors-cut rice', a selection of dishes piled high over a plate of lovely fluffy rice and topped with curry sauce. Originating from Hainanese Chinese descendants, the dish can be seen as a cross between a Malaysian *nasi lemak* and a Japanese katsu curry. The 'scissors' come from the Crispy Cream Cracker Pork (see page 60), traditionally for which pork shoulder steaks were freshly cut to order using a pair of meat scissors.

1. Wash the rice at least 3 times. Place in a bowl and run under cold water, gently moving the rice grains between the tips of your fingers and pouring the rice through a sieve in between each wash, until the water runs clear. Sieve one last time and set aside.

2. Mix the sauce ingredients together in a jug.

3. **Build Your Wok Clock:** Start at 12 o'clock with the rice, followed by the onion, ginger and garlic, the spices, green chillies, potato, the sauce, chicken stock and lastly the okra.

4. Place the rice in a saucepan with the measured water. Cover with a tight-fitting lid, place on a medium-high heat and bring to a vigorous boil. Then reduce the heat to low and simmer with the lid on for 12–15 minutes until the liquid has evaporated to the point where you start to see air pockets form in between some of the rice grains. Replace the lid, turn the heat off and leave the rice to sit for another 15 minutes or so until ready to serve.

5. Once the rice is cooking, heat 1–2 tablespoons of vegetable oil in a saucepan to a medium heat, add the onion and fry for 2–3 minutes. Add the ginger and garlic and fry for a minute or so. Then add all the spices together, the green chillies and potato in turn, frying for about a minute after each addition. Pour in one-quarter of the sauce and bring to a vigorous boil. Add another quarter of the sauce and again bring to a boil, then repeat this process until all the sauce has been added. Bring to a boil once again, pour in the chicken stock and cook on a medium heat for 20 minutes. Then add the okra and cook for 5–10 minutes before serving with the rice.

2 cups of jasmine rice (I use a 240ml/8½fl oz cup, holding 195g/7oz rice)
2 cups (see above) of water
1 onion, finely diced
½ thumb-sized piece of ginger, peeled and finely chopped
2 garlic cloves, finely chopped
3 green chillies, pierced with the tip of your knife
1 potato, peeled and cut into 5cm (2 inch) chunks
300ml (10fl oz) chicken stock
200g (7oz) okra (swapsies: green beans), cut into 3-4cm (1¼-1½ inch) lengths
vegetable oil

SAUCE
150ml (5fl oz) coconut milk
1 tablespoon sambal (swapsies: chilli bean sauce/toban jiang)
1 tablespoon light soy sauce
½ teaspoon salt

SPICES
2 star anise
1 cinnamon stick
1½ tablespoons curry powder

SINGAPOREAN

12 chicken wings
1 teaspoon five spice
½ teaspoon salt
3 star anise
1 small cinnamon stick
300ml (10fl oz) chicken stock
vegetable oil

SAUCE
6 tablespoons dark soy sauce
2 tablespoons Shaoxing rice
    wine (swapsies: dry sherry)
2 tablespoons soft brown sugar

STAR ANISE SOY WINGS

Soy sauce chicken has been a staple in my household for generations. It's the simplicity of using just a few ingredients to deliver a real punch of flavour that makes it one of my family's go-to dishes and such a crowd-pleaser. You'll often find this lightly spiced version on a plate of scissors-cut rice to balance out the crisp texture of the pork (see page 54).

1. Slice through the joints of the chicken wings to separate the flats and drums (the bony lower wing and the fleshier upper wing), then rub with the five spice and salt until well coated.

2. Mix the sauce ingredients together in a small bowl.

3. **Build Your Wok Clock:** Start at 12 o'clock with the spice-coated chicken wings, followed by the star anise, cinnamon stick, the sauce and lastly the chicken stock.

4. Heat 1 tablespoon of vegetable oil in a large saucepan on a medium-high heat until smoking hot. Add the chicken wings and sear on one side for 2–3 minutes. Flip the wings over and sear the other side for 2–3 minutes. Add the star anise and cinnamon and fry for another 1–2 minutes to infuse the spices and deepen the colour of the chicken skin.

5. Increase the heat to high, pour the sauce into the pan and bring to a vigorous boil. Stir the wings through the sauce, coating each piece while continuing to boil vigorously for 2–3 minutes. Pour in the chicken stock and bring to a boil again, then reduce the heat to medium and simmer for 20–30 minutes until the sauce has reduced by half, then serve.

CEREAL BUTTER PRAWNS

Here's a modern invention from Singapore and Malaysia that shows off what a melting pot of culinary culture Singapore truly is. The sweet-savoury nature of this crust will bring a satisfying crunch and lingering flavour to your meal. In Singapore this is always made with a particular brand of cereal, but I've swapped in instant oats here, which are easily available in supermarkets.

300–400g (10½–14oz) shell-on
  raw tiger prawns, peeled
4 tablespoons salted butter
3 garlic cloves, finely sliced
1–2 birds' eye chillies,
  roughly chopped
handful of fresh curry leaves
vegetable oil

MARINADE
1 tablespoon oyster sauce
¼ teaspoon white pepper
1 egg, well beaten
4 tablespoons cornflour

CRUST
100g (3½oz) instant oats
2 tablespoons milk powder
½ teaspoon sugar
½ teaspoon ground sea salt
¼ teaspoon white pepper

1. Butterfly the prawns by running a knife down the backs through the meat to open them out, then rinse under cold running water to remove the black digestive cord. Dab the prawns dry with kitchen paper. Mix the marinade ingredients together then massage the marinade into the prawns, adding the cornflour last, to create a sticky coating around each prawn.

2. Mix the crust ingredients together in a bowl.

3. **Build Your Wok Clock:** Start at 12 o'clock with 1 tablespoon of the butter, followed by the coated prawns, the rest of the butter, the garlic, chilli, curry leaves and lastly the crust ingredients.

4. Heat the 1 tablespoon of butter with 1 tablespoon of vegetable oil in a large frying pan to a medium-high heat. Once the butter is foaming, place the coated prawns, one at a time, in the pan so that they don't stick to each other and cook for 2–3 minutes until they turn coral pink in colour on the underside, then flip them over and fry until they are the same colour on the other side. Remove them from the pan.

5. Add the rest of the butter to the pan and again, heat until foaming, then add the garlic, chilli and curry leaves in quick succession and stir-fry for 30–60 seconds. Add the crust ingredients and stir-fry for 1–2 minutes. Return the prawns to the pan, fold through and stir-fry for 1–2 minutes until warmed through, then serve.

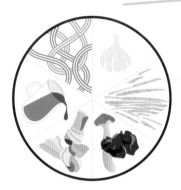

BRAISED NONYA NOODLES

As our very own School of Wok chef Cher often tells students, *chap chye* or *jap chae* brings a sense of nostalgia to many different Asian family feasts, as similar iterations of the dish can be found across the continent. This version is inspired by Nonya cuisine (a Peranakan community in Singapore, Malaysia and Indonesia). The tofu knots and the different types of dried mushrooms provide an earthiness and unique rustic and satisfying texture, replicating some of the qualities of meat, so there's no need to include any.

300g (10½oz) sweet potato noodles
handful of dried tofu knots
handful of dried wood ear mushrooms, soaked in hot water for at least 1 hour, then drained
6 dried shiitake mushrooms, soaked in hot water for at least 2 hours, preferably overnight, then drained
3 garlic cloves, finely chopped
4 Chinese leaf leaves, roughly chopped
vegetable oil
handful of coriander leaves, finely chopped, to garnish

STOCK
200ml (7fl oz) vegetable stock
1½ tablespoons soybean paste (swapsies: white miso paste)
1 tablespoon vegetarian stir-fry sauce (swapsies: oyster sauce)
1 teaspoon sesame oil
½ teaspoon sugar

1. Soak the sweet potato noodles in hot water for 15 minutes until they have softened and completely lost their packet shape, then drain.

2. Place the tofu knots in a saucepan filled with hot water, bring to a boil and boil for 10 minutes, then drain.

3. Squeeze any excess water out of the soaked mushrooms and then press firmly with kitchen paper to dry them. Slice the shiitake mushrooms.

4. Mix the stock ingredients together in a jug.

5. **Build Your Wok Clock:** Start at 12 o'clock with the garlic, followed by Chinese leaf, mushrooms, tofu knots, the stock and lastly the noodles.

6. Heat 1 tablespoon of vegetable oil in a saucepan or thick-based wok to a medium heat. Add the garlic and stir-fry for 30 seconds, then add the Chinese leaf, mushrooms and tofu knots in turn, stir-frying for 30 seconds after each addition. Increase the heat to high, pour in the stock and bring to a vigorous boil, then reduce the heat to medium and simmer for 15 minutes. Finally, add the noodles and boil for another 5 minutes. Garnish with the coriander and serve.

SINGAPOREAN

CRISPY CREAM CRACKER PORK

4 pork shoulder steaks
100g (3½oz) plain flour
2 tablespoons cornflour
1 egg
vegetable oil
Curry Sauce & Rice
   (see page 54), to serve

MARINADE
2 garlic cloves, finely chopped
½ teaspoon five spice
½ teaspoon salt
¼ teaspoon white pepper

CRUST
10 cream crackers
1 teaspoon salt
½ teaspoon sugar

The Chinese use of leftover dried pantry ingredients is inventive to say the least. I'm almost certain that dishes like this were created by a home chef not wanting to waste the last few cream crackers in the pack and felt the best way to make use of the stale contents of their tin was to deep-fry them (so often the creative culinary solution!). The pork is almost subsidiary to the crispy, slightly sweet and salty taste of the crust.

1. Bash the pork steaks with the back of a knife, a meat hammer or a rolling pin until flattened out and thin.

2. Mix the marinade ingredients together, then massage the marinade into the pork and leave to marinate for at least 30 minutes. For additional flavour, place the pork in a sealable food bag or on a tightly covered tray and refrigerate overnight.

3. For the crust, crush the cream crackers using a pestle and mortar, blitz them in a food processor to form a fine powder or place in a sealable food bag and bash with a rolling pin.

4. Set up 3 shallow bowls for dredging: mix the flour and cornflour together in one, beat the egg well in the second and mix the crust ingredients together in the third. Dip the marinated pork into the flour mixture until well coated and shake off any excess, then dip it into the beaten egg and let any excess drip off before dipping it into the crust ingredients, covering the meat completely. Set aside on a tray.

5. Half-fill a large saucepan, wok or deep-fryer with vegetable oil and bring to a medium-high heat. Test the temperature of the oil by placing the tip of a wooden chopstick or skewer in the oil. If it starts to fizz after a second or so, the oil has reached the desired temperature of around 180°C/350°F.

6. Carefully lay each pork escalope in the hot oil and deep-fry for 6–8 minutes until golden brown and floating at the top of the oil. Transfer to a plate lined with kitchen paper to drain the excess oil. Cut the escalopes into random strips and pieces with scissors and serve with the Curry Sauce & Rice.

SIZZLING EGG TOFU

One of the beauties of Singapore is that in between the skyscrapers and busy roads, in every little pocket of space, there are local restaurants and hawker centres, many established for decades. I remember one local hangout that completely changed my perception of tofu as a kid. By combining egg with the tofu, the edges crisp up when pan-fried, creating an irresistible melt-in-the-mouth texture.

200g (7oz) minced pork
3 dried shiitake mushrooms, soaked in hot water for at least 2 hours, preferably overnight, then drained
2 x 150g (5½oz) tubes of Japanese egg tofu (swapsies: firm silken tofu), sliced into 2cm (¾ inch) thick rounds
3 garlic cloves, finely chopped
2 spring onions, roughly chopped
vegetable oil

MARINADE
½ tablespoon oyster sauce
1 teaspoon sesame oil
1 teaspoon cornflour

SAUCE
200ml (7fl oz) chicken stock
1 tablespoon oyster sauce
1 tablespoon light soy sauce
1 tablespoon Shaoxing rice wine (swapsies: dry sherry)
½ teaspoon sugar

1. Mix the marinade ingredients together in a mixing bowl, then add the minced pork and massage the marinade into the meat.

2. Squeeze any excess water out of the soaked mushrooms and then press firmly with kitchen paper to dry them, then finely chop them.

3. Mix the sauce ingredients together in a jug.

4. **Build Your Wok Clock:** Start at 12 o'clock with the egg tofu, followed by the garlic and spring onions, shiitake mushrooms, marinated minced pork and lastly the sauce.

5. Heat 2 tablespoons of vegetable oil in a frying pan to a medium heat. Once hot, carefully place the egg tofu rounds in the oil and fry them for 3–4 minutes until golden brown on the underside. Then flip them over and fry until golden brown on the other side. Transfer to a plate lined with kitchen paper to drain the excess oil.

6. Heat 1 tablespoon of vegetable oil in a saucepan or thick-based pan (I like to use a clay pot or cast-iron wok here) to a medium heat. Add the garlic and spring onions and stir-fry for 30 seconds, then the shiitake mushrooms and stir-fry for 2–3 minutes until they start to crisp up around the edges. Add the minced pork and press onto the base of the pan with a spatula for 30 seconds or so to sear well, then start to chop into the meat with your spatula and stir-fry for 2–3 minutes. Increase the heat to high, and once the pan is smoking hot, pour in the sauce and bring to a vigorous boil. Add the fried egg tofu pieces, gently fold through the sauce and boil for 4–5 minutes until the sauce has thickened and begins to coat the ingredients, then serve.

S
I
N
G
A
P
O
R
E
A
N

GREEN KERABU SALAD

2 tablespoons desiccated
  coconut
100g (3½oz) green beans,
  trimmed and halved
300g (10½oz) spinach leaves
  (swapsies: nettles or
  edible fern)
2 tablespoons salted
  roasted peanuts

KERABU DRESSING
3–4 Thai shallots (swapsies:
  ½ red onion), finely sliced
½ thumb-sized piece of ginger,
  peeled and cut into
  matchsticks
3–4 lime leaves, finely sliced
2 birds' eye chillies, pierced
  with the tip of your knife
juice of 1 lime
4 tablespoons coconut water
½ teaspoon salt
1 tablespoon palm sugar
  (swapsies: soft brown sugar)

Pucuk paku is a specific type of fiddlehead fern that you'll often find in Malaysian and Singaporean cuisine. You'll also find different types of salads using these fiddleheads, where the dressing is a combination of sweet, sour and spicy flavours derived from lime juice, palm sugar and chilli. Similar to a good rendang, it is the combination of toasted desiccated coconut with the dressing that makes it so moreish and delicious. For ease and accessibility, I've used spinach here, but if you're a keen forager or just know the right people, this would work a treat with nettles or the traditional fiddlehead ferns if you can source them.

1. Toast the desiccated coconut in a dry frying pan on a medium heat for 4-5 minutes, stirring or tossing, until fragrant and uniformly golden brown. Allow to cool.

2. Blanch the beans in a saucepan of boiling water for 2-3 minutes, then remove with a slotted spoon and cool under cold running water. Blanch the spinach in the water for 1 minute, then drain and cool under cold running water. Once cooled, squeeze the excess water out of the spinach.

3. Mix the dressing ingredients together in a small bowl until the sugar fully dissolves.

4. Combine the beans and spinach with the dressing, toasted coconut and peanuts in a bowl and toss well to blend all the flavours, then serve.

S
I
N
G
A
P
O
R
E
A
N

TEOCHEW STEAMED FISH

2 sea bass fillets, with
   skin, descaled
½ thumb-sized piece of
   ginger, peeled and cut
   into matchsticks
2 garlic cloves, finely sliced
300g (10½oz) silken tofu, cut
   into 1–2cm (½–¾ inch) cubes
handful of mixed baby
   plum tomatoes
2–3 salted preserved plums,
   dried or in brine (optional)
handful of Chinese pickled
   mustard greens (*za cai*)
   (swapsies: gherkins),
   finely sliced
2 spring onions, cut
   into matchsticks
vegetable oil

SAUCE
2 tablespoons light soy sauce
1 tablespoon Shaoxing rice wine
   (swapsies: dry sherry)
½ teaspoon sugar
3–4 tablespoons hot water

Singapore has a large Teochew community, whose forebears will have originated from Chao Shan, a sea-adjacent region just northeast of Hong Kong. Given the location, fish unsurprisingly features prominently in the Teochew cuisine, and such a dish as this, served with some steamed rice, is a one-steam wonder, as it would make a wholesome meal by itself. The salted plums (found dried or brined in Asian supermarkets but can easily be omitted) add unique bittersweet and savoury tones to the sauce.

1. Place the fish fillets on a heatproof plate or tray to fit inside a bamboo steamer basket or your wok, then scatter the ginger and garlic over and around the fish. Then scatter around the silken tofu cubes, tomatoes, salted plums, if using, and pickled mustard greens.

2. Fill the wok about one-third up with boiling water and, if using, place the steamer holding the fish in the wok and cover the steamer with its lid. If you don't have a steamer, place a heatproof bowl in the middle of the wok, protruding just above the water's surface, then place the plate or tray of fish on top and cover the wok with its domed lid. Keep the water on a gentle boil to steam the fish for 8 minutes.

3. Meanwhile, mix the sauce ingredients together in a small bowl.

4. Turn the heat off under the wok, lift the lid of the steamer or wok and top the fish with the spring onions. Heat 1–2 tablespoons of vegetable oil in a wok or frying pan to smoking point, pour this over the spring onions and then pour the sauce over the top. Serve immediately.

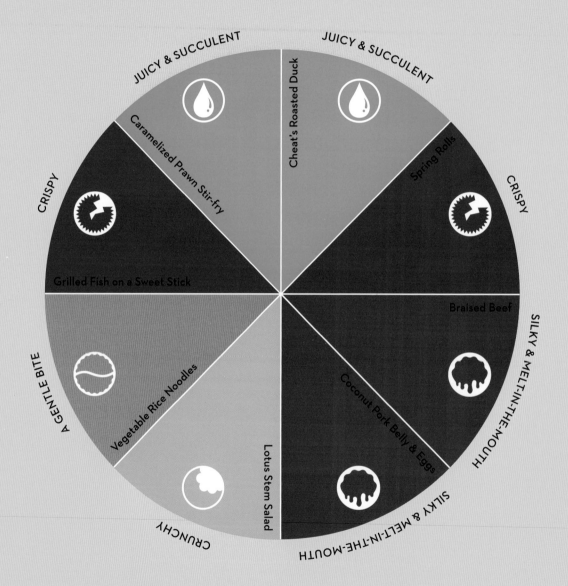

JUICY & SUCCULENT

JUICY & SUCCULENT

Cheat's Roasted Duck

Caramelized Prawn Stir-fry

Spring Rolls

CRISPY

CRISPY

Grilled Fish on a Sweet Stick

Braised Beef

SILKY & MELT-IN-THE-MOUTH

A GENTLE BITE

Coconut Pork Belly & Eggs

Vegetable Rice Noodles

SILKY & MELT-IN-THE-MOUTH

Lotus Stem Salad

CRUNCHY

VIETNAMESE

Moving south of Yunnan province in China is the top of South East Asia where the people, culture and cooking quickly change. Down the Red River to Hanoi in northern Vietnam, rice paper spring rolls (see page 80) and warming soup noodles are plentiful. The use of aromatic spices, steaming hot stews and colourful colanders full of well-shaken herbs is popular throughout the country. Through Vietnam's centre, chilli and the heartier spices are used more freely; venture south and deeper into the warmer climate, and cooling salads with sweet and sour flavours become more prevalent.

At School of Wok we have been lucky enough to join a few trips around South East Asia, and Thomas Nguyen, our wonderful tour guide, speaks passionately about the importance of food in Vietnamese culture and its role in bringing people together. As soon as I started writing this book I called Thomas to ask what would be his eight chosen dishes. Three hours later, talking into the early hours of his Hanoi morning, he was still reeling off his list and explaining why each dish is so important.

Food is ingrained in Vietnamese culture and the Vietnamese take no issue with the influence other cuisines have had on it, which is an inevitability given the various empires and people that have occupied the country throughout its history. While he certainly doesn't condone war and conflict, Thomas and his peers try to accept their recent history as a way of honouring what older generations have endured, and this includes taking a certain amount of pride in how Vietnamese food is prepared and the creative ways in which it has interacted with the cuisines of other cultures. Certain foods and cooking techniques from French, Chinese and American cuisines have seamlessly made their way into modern-day Vietnam life, creating an ever-changing bold and unique cuisine.

Thomas argues that if any meal is to be considered a feast within Vietnamese culture, it better be BIG. There should be as many dishes as possible on the table for a proper get together, a mentality that rings true in my own family, which is perhaps why Thomas and I have become fast friends. With this in mind, it was hard to pick a small selection of recipes to showcase here – I felt truly spoiled for choice.

Thomas advises that a showstopper roast meat will deliver the wow factor, alongside which you can balance out the table with fresher dishes including braised stews and herby salads. In Western cuisines these might be seen just as side dishes, but in Vietnamese tradition they are given an equal amount of respect as the main attraction, served in a generous manner alongside a punch of sweet and sour from additional sauces. Remember, colour and crunch are key factors in a Vietnamese feast, working to showcase other deeper flavours and softer, rich textures.

Let the Cheat's Roasted Duck marinate for as long as possible so that the skin will dry out nicely and become super-crispy while roasting. These Spring Rolls also need preparing well in advance to allow plenty of time for the sticky rice paper to dry out – just ensure there's nothing wet in the fridge that will add moisture and ruin them if leaving them there overnight! The Braised Beef and Coconut Pork Belly & Eggs can both be started early too, and then there will be a nice pause to make your Lotus Stem Salad. The many elements of the Vegetable Rice Noodles take a bit of time, so are best tackled next, leaving the Grilled Fish on a Sweet Stick closer to the finish to serve as fresh as possible, saving the Caramelized Prawn Stir-fry to last to avoid overcooking.

4 large eggs at room
  temperature
5–6 Thai shallots (swapsies:
  2 brown shallots), cut
  into wedges
4–5 garlic cloves, finely sliced
1 teaspoon black peppercorns
1kg (2lb 4oz) pork belly,
  cut into large chunks
500g (1lb 2oz) pork ribs,
  separated
2–3 tablespoons fish sauce,
  to taste
coconut oil or vegetable oil

SYRUP

3 tablespoons palm sugar
  (swapsies: soft brown sugar)
100ml (3½fl oz) coconut water
2 tablespoons dark soy sauce

STOCK

500ml (18fl oz) coconut water
500ml (18fl oz) chicken stock

COCONUT PORK BELLY & EGGS

The Vietnamese have mastered the art of melt-in-the-mouth braised dishes with sauces perfect to mop up with a bowl of rice or vermicelli. I wouldn't necessarily cook this and the Braised Beef (see page 78) for the same feast, but I wanted to showcase the glory of Vietnamese meaty stews.

1. Boil the eggs in a saucepan of boiling water for 7 minutes. Drain, run under cold water to cool enough to peel, then submerge in cold water to cool fully. Peel, halve and set aside.

2. For the syrup, melt the palm sugar in a saucepan on a medium-high heat until bubbling but not burning. Pour in the coconut water, bring to a vigorous boil and continue boiling for 3–4 minutes until the syrup reaches the consistency of maple syrup or runny honey. Remove from the heat and then scrape into a small bowl.

3. Mix the stock ingredients together in a large jug.

4. **Build Your Wok Clock:** Start at 12 o'clock with the shallots, followed by the garlic, black peppercorns, the syrup, pork belly and ribs, the stock, boiled eggs and lastly the fish sauce.

5. Heat 1–2 tablespoons of coconut oil or vegetable oil in a clay pot or large saucepan to a medium heat, add the shallots and fry for 1–2 minutes. Then add the garlic and fry for 30 seconds or so. Add the black peppercorns, then pour in the syrup and bring to a vigorous boil. Once the liquid has reduced slightly and starts to get a little stickier, add the pork belly and ribs and fold through, coating each piece of pork with the syrup. As the pork starts to caramelize and brown, pour over the stock, giving the bottom of the pan a good scrape with a wooden spoon or spatula to deglaze, and bring to a vigorous boil. Then reduce the heat to low, cover with a lid and simmer for 45 minutes. Remove the lid and simmer for another 45 minutes until tender.

6. Increase the heat to medium and remove the lid. Add the eggs, covering each one well in the sauce, and bubble away on a medium heat for 20–30 minutes, reducing and caramelizing the sauce again until it reaches the same syrupy consistency as before. Season to taste with the fish sauce and serve.

CHEAT'S ROASTED DUCK

8 duck legs

MARINADE
½ tablespoon ground turmeric
2 teaspoons ground cumin
2 teaspoons black pepper
1 teaspoon salt
2 tablespoons fish sauce
1 tablespoon oyster sauce

SA TÉ SAUCE
5–6 Thai shallots (swapsies:
   2 brown shallots)
1 head of garlic, cloves
   separated and peeled
½ thumb-sized piece of
   galangal or ginger, peeled
2 lemon grass stalks, trimmed
   and bruised
2 large red chillies
1 birds' eye chilli
3–4 tablespoons vegetable oil
½ teaspoon salt
1 teaspoon sugar
1½ tablespoons light soy sauce

Having a whole roast bird on the table is a ritual in many cultures, but anything bigger than a large chicken can be daunting. I've made my version of *vit quay* (roast duck) more manageable while hopefully staying true to the traditional flavours – the colour and crispness of the skin are most important.

1. Run a knife blade down the length of the drumstick of each duck leg to butterfly the leg meat but keep it attached to the bone.

2. Blanch the duck legs in a large saucepan of boiling water for 3–4 minutes. Drain and them run under cold water to cool. Dab dry with kitchen paper and place in a roasting tray.

3. Mix the marinade ingredients together, then rub the marinade all over the skin of each duck leg.

4. For the *sa té* sauce, finely chop the shallots, garlic, galangal or ginger, lemon grass and chillies or roughly chop and then pulse in a food processor to a coarse paste. Heat the vegetable oil in a wok or saucepan to a medium heat. Add the sauce mixture and fry for 8–10 minutes until aromatic and deeper in colour. Add the remaining ingredients and fry for another 4–5 minutes, then cool.

5. Massage 2 tablespoons of the *sa té* sauce into the meat side of the duck, trying not to get any on the skin. Set aside the rest of the sauce to serve for dipping.

6. Cover the duck with another roasting tray – I use a perforated tray to allow as much air to circulate the duck as possible. If you haven't got a big enough second tray, use a sheet of foil pierced with a few holes. Place in the fridge overnight.

7. Remove the duck from the fridge and leave it to come up to room temperature for 30 minutes before preheating the oven to 130°C/300°F/Gas Mark 2. Dab the skin of the duck with kitchen paper, place on a grill tray and roast for 2 hours. Increase the oven temperature to 210°C/450°F/Gas Mark 8 and roast for another 15 minutes to crisp up the skin. Serve with the *sa té* sauce on the side.

BRAISED BEEF

Bo kho is a cheering and hearty dish fit for any family feast. With carrots and potatoes featuring in the stew, this is a fantastic recipe for using up roast dinner leftovers if you fancy something different. I can see why my friend Thomas would always have this on his table for his family and friends; it's like a warm, beefy hug in a bowl.

600g (1lb 5oz) beef brisket in
    4cm (1½ inch) thick pieces
1 onion, cut into wedges
1 lemon grass stalk, trimmed,
    bruised and cut into thirds
4 star anise
1 cinnamon stick
1 teaspoon Chinese five spice
5 tomatoes, roughly chopped
½ teaspoon salt
3 carrots, in bite-sized chunks
3 potatoes, peeled and in
    bite-sized chunks
vegetable oil

PASTE

5–6 Thai shallots (swapsies:
    1 red onion), finely diced
4 garlic cloves, finely chopped
2 lemon grass stalks, trimmed,
    bruised and finely chopped
1 birds' eye chilli, finely chopped
½ thumb-sized piece of ginger,
    peeled and finely chopped

STOCK

1 litre (1¾ pints) chicken stock
1½ tablespoons fish sauce
½ tablespoon palm sugar
    (swapsies: soft brown sugar)

TO GARNISH

1 lime, cut into wedges
1 red chilli, finely sliced
handful of coriander leaves

1. Pound the paste ingredients together using a pestle and mortar, adding them one at a time, or blitz them in a food processor to form a smooth paste (you may need to add a tablespoon or so of water if using a machine).

2. Mix the stock ingredients together in a jug, stirring until the sugar has melted.

3. **Build Your Wok Clock:** Start at 12 o'clock with the paste, followed by the beef, onion, lemon grass, star anise, cinnamon stick, five spice, tomatoes, salt, the stock and lastly the carrots and potatoes.

4. Heat 1–2 tablespoons of vegetable oil in a saucepan to a medium heat. Add the paste and fry for 3–4 minutes until fragrant. Then add the beef, increase the heat to high to seal in the moisture and flavour and fry for 1–2 minutes without moving to get some caramelization on the meat. Then continue working around the wok clock up until the tomatoes, adding each ingredient in turn and stir-frying for 30 seconds or so after each addition. Add the tomatoes and salt, cover the pan with a lid and reduce the heat to medium to allow their juices to be released. Cook for 5–6 minutes, then remove the lid and stir well, scraping the bottom of the pan with a wooden spoon or spatula to release all the flavour of the paste.

5. Pour in the stock and bring to a boil, then reduce the heat to medium-low, cover with the lid again and simmer for at least 2½ hours – the longer you stew the meat, the more tender it will become – topping it up with water if required. Add the carrots and potatoes 45 minutes before serving and your stew will start to thicken while the carrots and potatoes cook. Serve garnished with the lime wedges, red chilli and coriander.

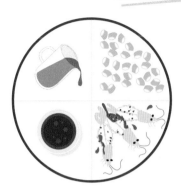

600g (1lb 5oz) shell-on
    raw tiger prawns
2 spring onions, roughly
    chopped into chunks
100ml (3½fl oz) chicken stock
vegetable oil

MARINADE

½ red onion, finely chopped
1 large red chilli, finely chopped
3 garlic cloves, finely chopped
½ teaspoon salt
½ teaspoon black pepper
1 tablespoon oyster sauce

SAUCE

2 tablespoons fish sauce
1 teaspoon dark soy sauce
1½ tablespoons brown sugar

CARAMELIZED PRAWN STIR-FRY

Consider this the Vietnamese version of sweet and sour prawns, known as *tom rim*, with a tweak. Here you'll find less emphasis on the sour flavour, so it's more sweet and salty in line with the snacking trend that continues to spread across the globe in various forms. The prawn shells for this dish are kept on and are supposed to be cooked to provide an extra crunchy texture to your feast. If you would rather prepare this dish with peeled prawns, it will still work, but I urge you to try crunching into the prawns with the shell intact for the full effect – the caramelized sauce will weave its way into every part of them.

1. Cut the tops of the prawn heads off (just under the eyes) with kitchen scissors and remove the legs. Use a cocktail stick or wooden skewer to remove the black digestive cord by poking it through the body of each prawn and pulling upwards in between the seams of the shell. Place the prepared prawns in a bowl.

2. Mix the marinade ingredients together, then rub the marinade into each prawn still with their shells on. Leave to marinate for at least 15–20 minutes in the fridge.

3. Mix the sauce ingredients together in a small bowl.

4. **Build Your Wok Clock:** Start at 12 o'clock with the spring onions, followed by the marinated prawns, the sauce and lastly the chicken stock.

5. Heat 1 tablespoon of vegetable oil in a wok to a medium-high heat until smoking hot, then add the spring onions and stir-fry for 30 seconds. Increase the heat to high, add the marinated prawns and stir-fry for 1–2 minutes. Pour in the sauce, bring to a vigorous boil and stir-fry for another minute. Then stop stirring and allow the prawns to sizzle and the heat to build. Once the wok is smoking hot again, pour in the chicken stock, bring to a vigorous boil and fold through every 15–20 seconds, continuing to stir-fry for another 1–2 minutes until all the sauce has caramelized and coated the prawns. Tip into a serving bowl and serve immediately.

SPRING ROLLS

1 pack of rice paper wraps
(about 16), softened just
before using in a bowl of hot
water by holding with both
hands above the bowl, then
dipping into and swivelling
them in the water until
soaked and softened.
Repeat with all the wraps.
vegetable oil
coriander sprigs, to serve

FILLING
1 garlic clove, finely chopped
300g (10½oz) minced pork
1 carrot, grated
handful of dried wood ear
mushrooms, soaked in hot
water for at least 1 hour,
then drained and finely
chopped (swapsies: dried
shiitake mushrooms)
nest of mung bean glass
vermicelli, soaked in hot
water for 2-3 minutes, then
drained and finely chopped
½ teaspoon salt
½ teaspoon sugar
½ teaspoon white pepper
1 tablespoon fish sauce

NUOC CHAM
1 garlic clove, finely chopped
1 birds' eye chilli, finely chopped
2 tablespoons fish sauce
2 tablespoons palm sugar
(swapsies: soft brown sugar)
4 tablespoons water
juice of ½ lime

As **Thomas quite rightly says, something deep-fried always goes down well when feeding a large group. The salty flavour draws you in, but it's the crispy, crunchy, slightly bubbled-up and chewy texture of deep-fried Vietnamese rice paper that fuels the obsession. You will want to cook these in small batches, at least for the first fry, as they can stick to each other. Believe me, it's worth the wait.**

1. Mix the filling ingredients together with your hands.

2. To make each roll, lay a soaked wrap on a chopping board and place 2 tablespoons of the filling towards the bottom third of the wrap. Gently roll the wrap forwards over the filling until you reach the middle. Fold the wrap sides in and continue to roll up and tighten the wrap into a neat cylinder. Place the rolls on a wire rack and leave uncovered to air-dry for at least 2 hours, or ideally overnight in the fridge. This ensures that the wraps dry out enough to prevent them from sticking when frying, but also makes them lovely and crispy once fried.

3. Mix the *nuoc cham* ingredients together in a small bowl.

4. Fill a wok one-third with oil and bring to a medium-high heat. Test the temperature by placing the tip of a wooden chopstick in the oil. If it starts to fizz after a second, the oil has reached the desired temperature. Carefully add 3-4 spring rolls to the hot oil one at a time at about 30-second intervals, placing them apart in the wok to prevent them from sticking to each other. Once the first batch has been added, reduce the heat to low and pop any bubbles in the wraps with the end of your chopstick or skewer as they bulge up. Fry for 4-5 minutes until cooked through, then remove with a slotted spoon or bamboo strainer and place on a wire rack or grill rack to drain the excess oil. Continue until all the spring rolls have been fried once.

5. When ready to serve, reheat the oil to a medium-high heat, when your chopstick or skewer starts to fizz after 3-4 seconds. Fry the spring rolls for about a minute each until crisp, in batches if necessary depending on the size of your wok. Drain on kitchen paper and serve with the coriander and the nuoc cham for dipping.

VIETNAMESE

80

VEGETABLE RICE NOODLES

350g (12oz) firm tofu
300g (10½oz) thick rice
    vermicelli (swapsies: sweet
    potato noodles)
1 carrot, peeled into ribbons
    with a vegetable peeler
    or cut into matchsticks
1 cucumber, peeled into ribbons
    with a vegetable peeler
    or cut into matchsticks
vegetable oil
handful of coriander,
    leaves picked
small handful of Thai
    basil leaves
small handful of mint leaves

MARINADE
2 tablespoons palm sugar
    (swapsies: soft brown sugar)
1 large shallot, finely chopped
3 tablespoons fish sauce
¼ teaspoon black pepper

SAUCE
4 tablespoons fish sauce
4 tablespoons rice vinegar
2 teaspoons palm sugar
    (swapsies: soft brown sugar)
200ml (7fl oz) vegetable stock
1 red Thai chilli, finely chopped
1 garlic clove, finely chopped
generous squeeze of lime juice

I love the ways in which dish names are typically derived throughout many Asian countries because they tend to run to extremes. Either they're named in reference to a very specific story or legend behind them or they're a literal description of what's on the plate. The latter makes it so much easier to understand what you might be ordering in a traditional restaurant even if you have no idea how to speak most of the language. This dish is called *bun chay* in Vietnamese, *bun* being the word for rice noodles, a significant staple of Vietnamese cuisine. Whatever word *bun* is followed by will indicate the type of topping on the noodles, in this instance *chay* meaning vegetables. So there you have it, a vegetable noodle dish for you to enjoy on its own or as the perfect accompaniment to any Vietnamese feast.

1. Carefully slice the tofu into 5mm (¼ inch) thick pieces or batons. Mix the marinade ingredients together then rub the marinade into the tofu.

2. For the sauce, add the fish sauce, rice vinegar, palm sugar and vegetable stock to a bowl and mix well until the sugar has dissolved. Then add the chilli and garlic along with the lime juice.

3. Add 1 teaspoon of vegetable oil to a frying pan on a medium-high heat, add the tofu and fry for about 3–4 minutes on each side until caramelized and crispy, pouring any excess marinade over the tofu.

4. Meanwhile, cook the vermicelli in a saucepan of boiling water for about 3–4 minutes until tender, then drain and briefly run under cold water to stop the cooking process and cool the noodles until they are just slightly warmer than room temperature.

5. To assemble your salad, place the noodles in a bowl. Pour 1–2 teaspoons of the sauce over them and mix to build the flavour. Add your vegetables to the bowl, followed by the crispy warm tofu. Top with the fresh herbs, dress with the sauce and serve.

GRILLED FISH ON A SWEET STICK

3 sugar cane sticks (swapsies:
 1–2 pineapple cores) per fish
1 whole red snapper or 2 whole
 sea bream, about 1kg (2lb 4oz)
 in total, cleaned, gutted
 and descaled
½ thumb-sized piece of ginger,
 peeled and finely sliced
3–4 Thai shallots (swapsies:
 1 brown shallot), finely sliced
3–4 garlic cloves, finely sliced
vegetable oil

DIPPING SAUCE
3 garlic cloves, finely chopped
3 tablespoons fish sauce
1 tablespoon palm sugar
 (swapsies: soft brown sugar)
1 tablespoon tamarind
 concentrate
4–5 tablespoons water

Roadside grills can often be found roaming the streets of Saigon offering passers-by lines of fish on sticks of sugar cane. The sticks are usually used to turn the fish as well as add sweetness to the naturally sweet flesh of the fish. Sold with a quick ladle of sauce in a bag, the seasoning itself is as simple as the whole set-up sounds. Recreating this dish at home without access to fresh sugar cane could present some difficulties (though it can often be found online), but if that's what's stopping you from giving it a try, the core of a pineapple makes a great alternative.

1. If using a pineapple core, slice it lengthways to create 3 thinner sticks that will fit inside the cavity of your fish. If using sugar cane, you may also need to chop through the sticks so that they will fit. Shave the ends of your sticks into pencil-like points so that you can push them through the cavity of the fish easily.

2. Make 3 evenly spaced incisions inside the cavity of the fish and then push your sticks through the cavity of the fish all the way up into the meat. Then stuff the ginger, shallots and garlic into the rest of the cavity and 'sew' it up by roughly weaving a bamboo skewer through the base of the cavity.

3. Mix the dipping sauce ingredients together in a ramekin or small bowl.

4. The ideal way to cook the fish is on a barbecue for about 8–10 minutes on each side, charring the skin of the fish to the point where it can literally be shaved off into ashes before you dig into the soft, sweet flesh.

5. If cooking inside, preheat the oven on the grill function to 220°C/425°F. Place the fish in a roasting tray lined with foil and brush the skin on both sides with vegetable oil. Grill the fish on the middle shelf for 10–12 minutes until charred on the top side, then turn the fish over and grill the other side for another 10–12 minutes. If you want to char the fish skin more, move the roasting tray to the top shelf to grill for another 1–2 minutes just before serving. Serve with the dipping sauce on the side.

LOTUS STEM SALAD

200g (7oz) fresh lotus stem
(swapsies: pickled lotus stem
or asparagus), chopped
on the diagonal
3–4 celery sticks, cut into
4–5cm (1½–2 inch) lengths
handful of mint, leaves picked
handful of Thai sweet basil,
leaves picked
handful of coriander or
Vietnamese sawtooth
coriander, leaves picked
½ handful of roasted salted
peanuts, coarsely crushed

CLASSIC PICKLE
1 carrot, cut into matchsticks
½ small daikon, peeled and
cut into matchsticks
2 tablespoons rice vinegar
1 teaspoon salt
½ teaspoon sugar

DRESSING
1 garlic clove, finely chopped
3–4 tablespoons water
2 tablespoons vegetarian fish
sauce (swapsies: light soy
sauce or fish sauce)
juice of 1 lime wedge
1 tablespoon sugar

This salad is usually tossed with blanched prawns and slow-poached pork shoulder, but the flavours are just as delicious on their own. Fresh lotus stem can be a tricky ingredient to find, although it is available from some Thai and Vietnamese online supermarkets, and jarred pickled versions are also available more readily. Lotus stem is similar to, but not to be confused with, the thicker, hardier lotus root. It absorbs liquid and flavour incredibly well, while retaining a good crunch. If you can't find lotus stem, asparagus makes a simple, accessible alternative. Either way, this is super-tasty and a fantastic counterbalance to the rest of the dishes in this chapter.

1. Mix the classic pickle ingredients together, allowing the carrot and daikon to sit in the rice vinegar mixture for at least 1 hour, or preferably in a sterilized airtight container overnight in the fridge.

2. Mix the lotus stem, celery and pickle together in a large bowl. Mix the dressing ingredients together in a small bowl until the sugar has dissolved, then dress the salad 15–20 minutes before serving. Scatter with the fresh herbs and crushed peanuts and serve with the classic pickle on the side.

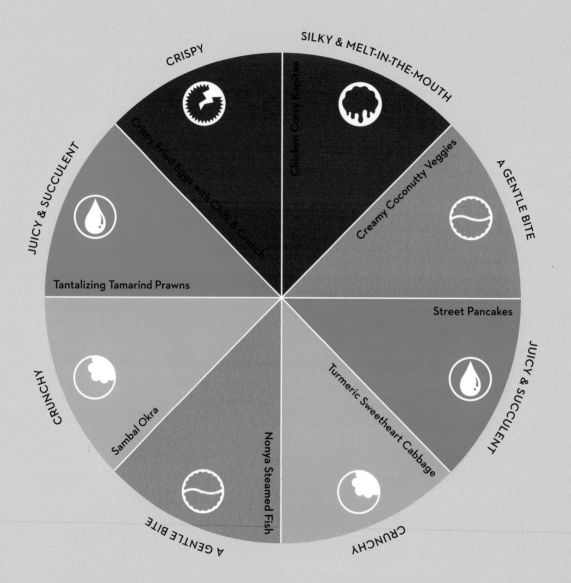

CRISPY

SILKY & MELT-IN-THE-MOUTH

JUICY & SUCCULENT

A GENTLE BITE

Crispy Fried Eggs with Chilli & Crunch

Chicken Curry Kapitan

Creamy Coconutty Veggies

Tantalizing Tamarind Prawns

Street Pancakes

CRUNCHY

JUICY & SUCCULENT

Sambal Okra

Turmeric Sweetheart Cabbage

Nonya Steamed Fish

A GENTLE BITE

CRUNCHY

MALAYSIAN

Whether in the bustling metropolises or tiny villages, Malaysia is a melting pot of hawker stands lining the streets and car parks. Any empty spaces that *can* be filled with food stalls *will* be filled with food stalls. There is a reverence for eating opportunities throughout the country, to such a degree that locals and tourists alike will willingly travel miles just to visit the roti stand, *popiah* pop-up, curry hut, *nasi lemak* vendor or kerbside kerabu seller that is rumoured to be the best of its kind in the country (see pages 98, 102 and 195 for some of my versions). I honestly feel that wherever you go in Malaysia, you are quite likely to stumble across the finest version of any particular dish, with each town or village stoking up that emotion of food euphoria once again. In my opinion, Malaysian food should have a far bigger billing on the world stage than it gets, and I do wonder why it doesn't have as much exposure in the West as some of its South East Asian counterparts like Thai or Vietnamese cuisine.

Putting together a cookbook is an exhausting process, though the rewards are so special that you can often forget those gruelling aspects. One of the biggest payoffs for me, aside from the joy of sharing food with people around the world, is the huge team effort that it takes to make a good cookbook and the satisfaction that we all get after a long day of photography. Throughout the production of this book, I have had the pleasure of working with what I now call my 'All Malaysian Food Stylo Milo' kitchen team, who have been cooking alongside chefs from the School of Wok. Yasmin and Gileng are both originally from Malaysia, and the glee on their faces when I told them that the cover for the book would picture a Malaysian feast was unforgettable. Spending time with these lovely Malaysian sisters reminds me of all my times in Malaysia, as they have such a naturally humble nature that resonates throughout their culture. Quietly confident, they seamlessly dish out feasts every photoshoot day, letting the smells coming from the kitchen speak for themselves as proof of their talents.

The dishes in this suggested feast are a combination of home-style Malaysian cooking and foods you are more likely to find on the streets. They are fun, flavourful, varied in their techniques and none of them take overly long to cook. There are dishes that represent the differing cultures that make up this melting pot of a cuisine, from Malay to Chinese, Peranakan (Nonya) and Indian, bringing an amazing balance to the table all at once. Dare I say it, you can even try mixing and matching some of the dishes from the Indonesian and Singaporean chapters to create multicultural feasts of your own!

As with most curries, the Chicken Curry Kapitan and Creamy Coconutty Veggies can both be cooked in advance and will sit well, so get them going first. Next, try the Street Pancakes, as they are best served at room temperature to retain a bit of crunch. Decidedly crunchy, the Turmeric Sweetheart Cabbage can be prepared in advance and served cold, or reheated for 1–2 minutes if you'd like it hot. Get your paste and sauce for the Nonya Steamed Fish ready, but put the fish on to steam just 10 minutes or so before serving the feast, then you can finish up prepping your Wok Clocks for your choice of Sambal Okra, Tantalizing Tamarind Prawns or Crispy Fried Eggs with Chilli & Crunch so that they can be served straight from the wok.

4–5 lime leaves
400ml (14fl oz) coconut milk
2 sweet potatoes, peeled and
    cut into large chunks
350ml (12fl oz) vegetable stock
200g (7oz) kale (swapsies:
    cavolo nero or large
    spinach leaves)
200g (7oz) green
    beans, trimmed
vegetable oil
sea salt

SPICE PASTE
1 red onion, finely chopped
2 garlic cloves, finely chopped
5–6 dried red chillies, soaked
    in hot water for 10–15
    minutes, then drained
    and finely chopped
1 lemon grass stalk, trimmed,
    bruised and finely chopped
4 tablespoons ready-made
    crispy fried onions or shallots

CREAMY COCONUTTY VEGGIES

The traditional form of this dish, *sayur lemak*, which literally translates as 'fatty vegetables', could easily be a little deceptive for a vegetarian, as it's often cooked with a generous spoonful of *belacan* (toasted shrimp paste) in the sauce. So here I've swapped out the shrimp paste for crispy fried onions to keep that essential boost of savoury flavour while making it vegan. Alternatively, if you aren't cooking for someone vegetarian, just replace the crispy fried onions with 1–2 teaspoons of *belacan* to transform the recipe back to its original flavours. In which case, you may as well throw in some raw peeled and deveined tiger prawns for the last 3–4 minutes of cooking for a little extra texture, too.

1. Pound the spice paste ingredients together using a pestle and mortar, adding them one at a time, or blitz them in a food processor to form a smooth paste (you may need a tablespoon of water).

2. **Build Your Wok Clock:** Start at 12 o'clock with the spice paste, followed by the lime leaves, coconut milk, sweet potatoes, vegetable stock, kale and lastly the green beans.

3. Heat 1–2 tablespoons of vegetable oil in a large saucepan to a medium heat. Add the spice paste, stir through the hot oil and fry for 4–5 minutes until aromatic and deeper in colour. Add the lime leaves and stir, then pour in one-quarter of the coconut milk, mix it into the paste and bring to a boil. Add another quarter of the coconut milk and again bring to a boil. Then add the sweet potatoes, fold through and allow the sauce to bubble up over the sweet potato pieces for 4–5 minutes. Pour in the rest of the coconut milk and bring to a boil once again, then add the vegetable stock and simmer for 20–25 minutes until the sweet potatoes are cooked through, reducing the heat if it begins to boil too vigorously.

4. Once the sweet potatoes are tender, add the kale to the curry and cook for 3–4 minutes, then add the green beans and cook for 3–4 minutes until they are just tender. Season with sea salt to taste and serve.

M
A
L
A
Y
S
I
A
N

94

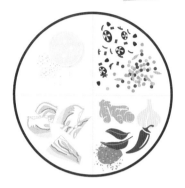

3 garlic cloves, finely sliced
½ thumb-sized piece of ginger,
    peeled and finely chopped
2 green chillies, pierced with
    the tip of your knife
handful of fresh curry
    leaves (optional)
1 sweetheart cabbage, roughly
    chopped into chunks
½ teaspoon salt
juice of ½ lemon
vegetable oil

WHOLE SPICES
3 large dried red chillies,
    soaked in hot water for
    10–15 minutes, then drained
    and roughly chopped
1 teaspoon mustard seeds
½ teaspoon cumin seeds

GROUND SPICES
2 teaspoons ground turmeric
½ teaspoon ground coriander
¼ teaspoon chilli powder

TURMERIC SWEETHEART CABBAGE

With the huge influence of Indian culture in Malaysia, there are certain dishes that are so simple and appealing, they can be found popping up across its different cuisines, whether to complement an Indian street meal or served alongside the coconut rice of a *nasi kandar* or *nasi lemak*. This recipe is my take on a chunkier version of a classic Gujarati *sambharo* — a type of quick-cook slaw that my mother-in-law says I cook more often than she does in her Indian home. I love it as a side or a main, or finely chopped up the next day in a cheese toastie. It's so veratile it could go with anything!

1. **Build Your Wok Clock:** Start at 12 o'clock with the whole spices, followed by the garlic, ginger, green chillies, curry leaves, if using, the ground spices, cabbage, salt and lastly the lemon juice.

2. Heat 1 tablespoon of vegetable oil in a thick-based wok to a medium heat, add the whole spices and cover with a lid. After a minute or so, the mustard seeds will start to pop, hitting the base of the lid. Once the popping has stopped, remove the lid, add the garlic, ginger, green chillies, curry leaves, if using, and the ground spices, adding each ingredient in turn and stir-frying for 15–20 seconds after each addition.

3. Add the cabbage to the wok, increase the heat to high and stir-fry for 4–5 minutes until tender but still with a slight bite. Season with the salt and lemon juice, then serve.

STREET PANCAKES

BATTER
250g (9oz) plain flour
1 tablespoon cornflour
1 teaspoon sea salt
350–375ml (12–13fl oz) cold water

FILLINGS
vegetable oil
1 turnip, peeled and grated
2 carrots, peeled and grated
¼ teaspoon salt
½ teaspoon sesame oil handful
    of beansprouts, rinsed
3 eggs (optional)
10–15 raw peeled tiger prawns,
    deveined (optional)
4-5 Romaine lettuce leaves,
    cut into 3–4 pieces
2 spring onions, cut
    into matchsticks
handful of salted roasted
    peanuts, roughly crushed
handful of crispy fried onions
    or shallots

SAUCES
hoisin sauce
sambal (ready-made
    or see page 122)

The traditional method of cooking these Malaysian pancakes, or *popiah*, is by 'punching' a handful of sticky dough onto a special crêpe-style hot plate, then pulling off the excess to leave a super-thin layer to crisp up. It takes some practise to finesse, so leave it to the professional street vendors and follow this much simpler method. I've gone for a traditional filling here, but leftover roast chicken and fresh salad, also works a treat. Just don't skimp on a good brush of the sauces!

1. For the batter, mix the dry ingredients together, then gradually whisk in the measured water until you have a smooth batter, the consistency of double cream.

2. For the fillings, heat ½ tablespoon of vegetable oil in a wok or saucepan to a high heat, add the turnip, carrots, salt and sesame oil and stir-fry for 1 minute. Transfer to a sieve to drain and cool.

3. Blanch the beansprouts in a saucepan of boiling water for 30 seconds, then remove them with a slotted spoon, drain and allow to cool. Add the eggs, if using, to the water and boil for 8 minutes, adding the prawns, if using, for the last 3–4 minutes to cook through. Drain and cool under cold running water. Peel the eggs and roughly chop them, and cut the prawns in half.

4. Heat a dry nonstick frying pan to a medium heat. Add 1 ladleful (125ml/4fl oz) of the batter to the middle of the pan and quickly spread it over the base with a brush to form a thin round pancake. Cook without touching for 1–2 minutes until the sides start to crisp up and come away from the base of the pan. Carefully lift one edge with your fingers or a spatula and then peel the pancake off the pan, place on a clean tea towel and cover with another tea towel. Repeat with the remaining batter, piling the pancakes on top of each other inside the tea towels as you go.

5. Lay each pancake in turn on a chopping board and brush with a generous amount of hoisin sauce and sambal, then add a couple of pieces of lettuce, followed by 1–2 tablespoons of each of the filling ingredients. Fold the pancake sides in, then fold the bottom up over the filling towards the middle and roll the pancake up. Slice in half and serve.

NONYA STEAMED FISH

4 thick trout or salmon
   fillets, with skin, descaled
vegetable oil
coriander sprigs, to garnish

SPICE PASTE
5–6 Thai shallots (swapsies:
   1 red onion), finely chopped
3 garlic cloves, finely chopped
3 large red chillies,
   finely chopped
2 lime leaves, finely chopped
½ thumb-sized piece of ginger,
   peeled and finely chopped
1 teaspoon black peppercorns

SAUCE
1 tablespoon fermented
   soybean paste (swapsies:
   red miso paste)
1 tablespoon oyster sauce
1 tablespoon sweet chilli sauce
½ tablespoon fish sauce
½ teaspoon soft brown sugar
50ml (2fl oz) vegetable
   or chicken stock

As with most fish dishes in Asia, the steamed fish in this kind of recipe would traditionally be kept whole and would usually be red snapper, sea bass or grouper. I love the deep colour from the saucy spice paste, known as *rempah*, which makes for a dramatic finish and always commands a big 'wow' from dinner guests when presenting it at the table. Here I've gone for trout or salmon fillets with their vibrant orangey-pink hue not only to colour match but also to complement the flavours.

1. Pound the spice paste ingredients together using a pestle and mortar, adding them one at a time, or blitz them in a food processor to form a smooth paste (you may need a tablespoon of water).

2. Mix the sauce ingredients together in a small bowl or jug.

3. Place the fish fillets skin-side up on a heatproof plate or tray to fit inside a bamboo steamer or your wok. Heat 1–2 tablespoons of vegetable oil in a wok or frying pan to a medium heat, add the paste and stir-fry for 4–5 minutes until aromatic and deeper in colour. Pour in the sauce, mix it into the paste and fry for 5–6 minutes until the liquid has mostly evaporated and the mixture has become paste-like in consistency. Spoon the cooked paste over the skin of the fish fillets.

4. Fill the wok about one-third up with boiling water and, if using, place the steamer holding the fish in the wok and cover the steamer with its lid. If you don't have a steamer, place a heatproof bowl in the middle of the wok, protruding just above the water's surface, then place the plate or tray of fish on top and cover the wok with its domed lid. Keep the water on a gentle boil to steam the fish for 8–10 minutes, depending on the thickness of the fillets. Garnish with the coriander and serve.

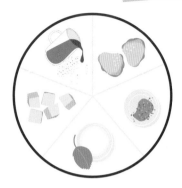

8 chicken thighs, with skin
    and bone
5–6 lime leaves
300ml (10fl oz) coconut milk
1 potato, peeled and cut
    into large chunks
300ml (10fl oz) chicken stock
vegetable oil
salt (optional)

MARINADE
2 teaspoons ground turmeric
1 teaspoon salt
juice of ¼ lime

CURRY PASTE
5 shallots, finely chopped
4–5 large red chilies, finely
    chopped
2 lemon grass stalks, trimmed,
    bruised and finely chopped
½ thumb-sized piece of
    galangal (swapsies: ginger),
    peeled and finely chopped
¼ thumb-sized piece of
    turmeric, peeled and finely
    chopped (swapsies:
    ½ teaspoon ground turmeric)
6 candlenuts (swapsies:
    macadamia nuts or
    blanched hazelnuts)
½ teaspoon *belacan* (toasted
    shrimp paste; swapsies:
    crispy fried onions)

CHICKEN CURRY KAPITAN

Name a curry 'The Captain's Curry', and no matter where it comes from, it's bound to sell. If the *kapitan* cooked it, you had better eat it up! This classic chicken curry is a Penang favourite. It's one of those dishes that is even tastier the next day, so if cooking it up for a big feast, consider making a double quantity the day before. As well as being more flavourful, it will be less stressful to have a whole dish made ahead of time, freeing you up to focus on preparing some of the speedier dishes on the day.

1. Mix the marinade ingredients together, then massage them into the chicken.

2. Pound the curry paste ingredients together using a pestle and mortar, adding them one at a time, or blitz them in a food processor to form a smooth paste (you may need a tablespoon of water).

3. **Build Your Wok Clock:** Start at 12 o'clock with the marinated chicken, followed by the curry paste, lime leaves, coconut milk, potato and lastly the chicken stock.

4. Heat 1–2 tablespoons of vegetable oil in a large saucepan or thick-based wok to a medium-high heat. Add the chicken thighs skin-side down and sear on one side for 3–4 minutes until golden brown, then flip over and sear the other side for 3–4 minutes to seal the chicken all over. Transfer the thighs to a plate.

5. Reduce the heat to medium, add the curry paste and fry for 4–5 minutes, folding the paste through the remaining oil while scraping any bits of chicken off the base. Add the lime leaves and fry for another minute or so. Pour in one-quarter of the coconut milk, mix it into the paste and bring to a boil. Add another quarter of the coconut milk and again bring to a boil, then repeat this process until all the coconut milk has been added.

6. Add the potato and seared chicken to the curry sauce and bring back to a boil, then pour the chicken stock over the chicken and bring to a boil one last time. Reduce the heat to medium and simmer for 30 minutes until the sauce is reduced by half. Season with a pinch of salt, if needed, before serving.

M
A
L
A
Y
S
I
A
N

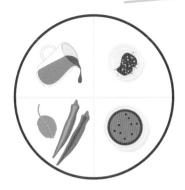

SAMBAL OKRA

Unlike some of the other feasts in the book, you'll notice the spice and heat theme running through most of the dishes in this chapter; a classic trait of Malaysian cuisine with its love for all things chilli. Don't be intimidated or put off by the notorious gooey texture of okra (ladies' fingers) – if stir-fried quickly and not overstewed in the sauce, the okra retains a bite that is absolutely delicious, and the slick ooziness works itself perfectly into the stickiness of the sambal. A simple, ideal accompaniment to the meaty curries or spicy fish dishes.

1. Pound the sambal paste ingredients together using a pestle and mortar, adding them one at a time, or blitz them in a food processor to a smooth paste (you may need to add a tablespoon or so of water if using a machine).

2. Mix the sambal liquid ingredients together in a small bowl.

3. Stir the salt into a bowl of water until dissolved. Slice each okra finger diagonally into 2–3 pieces, add to the salted water and leave until ready to add to the wok, then drain well.

4. **Build Your Wok Clock:** Start at 12 o'clock with the sambal paste, followed by the sambal liquid, lime leaves and okra and lastly the vegetable stock or water.

5. Heat 2–3 tablespoons of vegetable oil in a wok to a medium heat. Add the sambal paste, reduce the heat to low and fry for 6–7 minutes until highly aromatic and a deeper orangey-brown colour. Add the sambal liquid and stir-fry for 8–10 minutes until the liquid has evaporated and the mixture has become jammy in consistency. Increase the heat to high, add the lime leaves and okra and stir-fry for 1–2 minutes. Pour in the vegetable stock or water, bring to a vigorous boil and cook for 1–2 minutes, then serve.

½ teaspoon salt
300g (10½oz) okra, tops trimmed (swapsies: green beans, trimmed)
5–6 lime leaves
100ml (3½fl oz) vegetable stock or water
vegetable oil

SAMBAL PASTE
4–5 Thai shallots (swapsies: ½ red onion), finely sliced
2 large red chillies, finely chopped
2 dried red chilies, soaked in hot water for 10–15 minutes, then drained and finely chopped
2 garlic cloves, finely chopped
1 lemon grass stalk, trimmed, bruised and finely chopped
½ thumb-sized piece of galangal or ginger, peeled and finely chopped
1–2 teaspoons *belacan* (toasted shrimp paste) (swapsies: 2 tablespoons ready-made crispy fried onions or shallots)

SAMBAL LIQUID
1 tablespoon tamarind concentrate or lime juice
½ tablespoon dark soy sauce
½ teaspoon salt
½ teaspoon sugar

2 garlic cloves, finely sliced
10–15 large shell-on raw prawns
50ml (2fl oz) chicken or
   vegetable stock
vegetable oil
coriander sprigs, to garnish

SAUCE
4 tablespoons tamarind
   concentrate
1 tablespoon light soy sauce
½ tablespoon dark soy sauce
½ teaspoon sea salt
2 tablespoons palm sugar
   (swapsies: soft brown sugar)

TANTALIZING TAMARIND PRAWNS

Here's a recipe that packs a punch with very few ingredients.
The dish works a treat with regular raw tiger prawns, but if
you can get hold of any freshly caught whole prawns or similar
crustaceans, the juice from the heads and shells will add a
natural sweet-savoury flavour to the sauce that you just won't
be able to resist. Spanish red carabineros prawns, Atlantic red
tiger prawns or even Scottish langoustines will make the sauce
extra dreamy if you can find them. Anything local, fresh and
sustainable is my go-to for this very special treat.

1. Mix the sauce ingredients together in a small bowl until
the sugar fully dissolves.

2. **Build Your Wok Clock:** Start at 12 o'clock with the garlic,
followed by the prawns, the sauce and lastly the stock.

3. Heat 1–2 tablespoons of vegetable oil in a wok to a medium
heat, add the garlic and stir-fry for 30 seconds. Add the
prawns and press them down into the hot oil with a spatula
for 1–2 minutes, then flip them over and sear the other side
for 1–2 minutes.

4. Increase the heat to high and heat the oil until smoking hot.
Pour in the sauce and bring to a vigorous boil, then pour the
stock around the edges of the wok and fold the prawns through
the sauce. Continue boiling for 1–2 minutes until the sauce has
thickened enough to coat and almost wrap around the prawns,
then garnish with the coriander and serve.

4 eggs
vegetable oil
handful of raw peanuts,
   with skin (optional)
handful of dried anchovies
   (*ikan bilis*) (optional)

DRESSING
4 mixed red and green birds'
   eye chillies, roughly chopped
1 garlic clove, finely chopped
½ tablespoon soft brown sugar
3 tablespoons light soy sauce
1 tablespoon rice vinegar

CRISPY FRIED EGGS WITH CHILLI & CRUNCH

There are plenty of meat, fish, seafood and vegetable dishes in this chapter, but nothing particularly crispy yet. Often in Malaysian cuisine, the rice, curry or noodles will be topped with a crispy wok-fried egg, the savoury version of the cherry on the cake. This serves four but, for a satisfying but simple midweek meal, I'd recommend cooking any of the curries or veggie dishes (or even just rice if you're really short on time) and topping it off with this perfect mix of crisp and crunch.

1. Mix the dressing ingredients together in a small bowl or ramekin. You can store the dressing in an airtight container in the fridge for 3–4 days.

2. If using the peanuts and dried anchovies, heat 5–6 tablespoons of vegetable oil in a wok to a medium-high heat, add the peanuts and fry them for 3–4 minutes until the skins start to crisp up. Remove them with a slotted spoon and drain through a sieve. Repeat this process with the dried anchovies.

3. Heat 1–2 tablespoons of vegetable oil in a frying pan or wok to medium-high heat. Once smoking hot, crack 2 eggs in, keeping them separate, then reduce the heat to medium and carefully spoon some of the oil over the egg whites but not the yolks. Fry for about 2 minutes until the base of the egg is super-crispy and the egg white has bubbled up around the yolk. Transfer to a serving plate. Repeat this process.

4. Serve the crispy eggs with a drizzle of the dressing over the top, and the fried peanuts and anchovies on the side, if using.

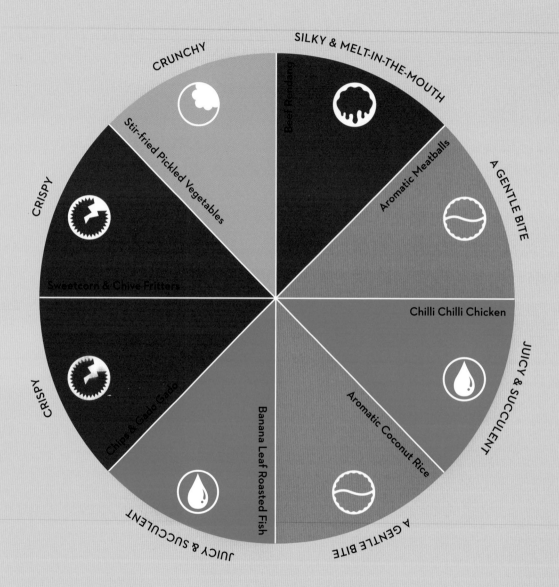

CRUNCHY

SILKY & MELT-IN-THE-MOUTH

Beef Rendang

Stir-fried Pickled Vegetables

A GENTLE BITE

CRISPY

Aromatic Meatballs

Sweetcorn & Chive Fritters

Chilli Chilli Chicken

CRISPY

JUICY & SUCCULENT

Chips & Gado Gado

Aromatic Coconut Rice

Banana Leaf Roasted Fish

JUICY & SUCCULENT

A GENTLE BITE

INDONESIAN

The first time I stepped foot in Indonesia, I was barely in my teens and was on a business trip to Jakarta with my dad. In writing this book, I've been jogging my memory of how this bustling city (and others) felt to me as a young Westernized Asian kid, having spent my first ten years in our little North London bubble. Weirdly, what I remember most is the mixture of smells: fumes from diesel buses filled to the brim, the aroma of slow-cooked rendang (see page 114) and the light citrusy smell of a rambutan being squished open in my hands for the first time. I also have vivid memories of metal baskets welded together at differing heights and spread over the back of a bicycle, ensuring each of the various deep-fried snacks within drained any excess oil away from the others. I loved this attention to detail where only the tarmac took the oily hit rather than any of the food being tainted. Indonesians have this ingenious way of making a food stand out of anything and their hawker stalls uniquely often take on the appearance of small huts, resting on the equivalent of a tricycle with supersized wheels. What's more, as in its neighbouring countries Malaysia and Singapore, Indonesia's hawker stalls offer some of the best eating experiences ever.

Lara Lee was one of the first students to enrol on a long-term School of Wok course, and she later wrote the widely regarded *Coconut & Sambal* cookbook, which pays tribute to her Indonesian background, the culture and the cuisine. I asked Lara what her perfect feasting dishes would be: 'We Indonesians *love* to eat food that stimulates all the senses, not just taste, especially noting the sounds that we make when we are eating. It's something that we often bypass but shouldn't. The sound of crunching into something crispy and deep-fried, for example, stimulates your appetite just as much as any flavours you'll taste.' Lara's right and that's why those deep-fried snack bikes are key to the cuisine. The satisfaction we get from the crunching sound and crispy texture is just as good as the taste itself, setting the pace for the entire meal. As Lara points out: 'Without something deep-fried and crispy on a tableful of food, our brains wouldn't have a good gauge as to how melt-in-the-mouth, succulent or juicy another dish really is.' Contrast is central to enjoyment, which is perhaps why deep-fried food always tastes so good, especially when followed by a different texture, which then highlights the benefits of both.

When making your Indonesian feast, the Beef Rendang takes time – the longer the better – so make this on a day you can give it the love it deserves. It freezes well, so you could even cook a massive batch and freeze it in smaller portions. Making meatballs can be a little faffy, so it's worth getting your Aromatic Meatballs prepared early. Once poached, they are easy to warm up and generous in their resilience if cooked a bit longer than suggested too. Chilli Chilli Chicken also takes in more flavour the longer it sits covered in all the chillies and their glory, so you can have this prepared beforehand and just reheat it for 10 minutes when ready to serve. The Aromatic Coconut Rice is to die for and will be the anchor for your whole feast, so tackle that next. The Banana Leaf Roasted Fish dish can all be prepared in advance and popped into the oven 20 minutes before serving your meal. Then you can turn your attention to the deep-fried dishes, either Chips & Gado Gado or the Sweetcorn & Chive Fritters – I'd recommend just one of these so that you can focus solely on it while deep-frying and without the risk of running out of hob space. That said, you can prepare the ingredients for the veggies, sauce or batter in advance too. For that vital noisy crunch and sweet and sour tang, the simple Stir-fried Pickled Vegetables will balance your meal right at the end of your feast cooking time.

BEEF RENDANG

A good rendang could take its place in a few of these chapters, with Malay, Singaporean and Indonesian hawkers all valid contenders for the rendang world championships. The toasted coconut in this version gets me excited, as cooking desiccated coconut completely changes the base flavour of the curry while adding a unique and perfectly viscous consistency to the sauce, allowing it to stick to every inch of the tender curried meat and making each mouthful that much more flavourful. Serve with rice on the side.

1 tablespoon ground turmeric
1 teaspoon chilli powder
800g (1lb 12oz) beef shin, cut
    into 5cm (2 inch) chunks
5–6 tablespoons desiccated
    coconut
1 lemon grass stalk, trimmed,
    bruised and halved
    lengthways
6–10 lime leaves
coriander leaves, roughly
    chopped, to garnish

CURRY PASTE
10 dried red chillies, soaked
    in hot water for 10–15 minutes,
    then drained, deseeded and
    finely chopped
5 Thai shallots (swapsies: 1 large
    red onion), finely chopped
3 lemon grass stalks, trimmed,
    bruised and finely chopped
5 garlic cloves, finely chopped
½ thumb-sized piece of
    galangal or ginger, peeled
    and finely chopped

STOCK
400ml (14fl oz) can coconut milk
200ml (7fl oz) chicken stock
    or water
1 tablespoon tamarind paste
1 tablespoon palm sugar
    (swapsies: soft brown sugar)
1 teaspoon sea salt, or to taste

1. Massage the turmeric and chilli powder into the beef.

2. Pound the curry paste ingredients together using a pestle and mortar, adding them one at a time, or blitz them in a food processor to form a smooth paste (you may need to add a tablespoon or so of water if using a machine).

3. Toast the desiccated coconut in a dry frying pan on a medium heat for 4–5 minutes, stirring or tossing, until fragrant and uniformly golden brown. Allow to cool. You can then blitz it in a food processor to form a fine powder, if you like, for a really smooth sauce.

4. Mix the stock ingredients together in a jug.

5. **Build Your Wok Clock:** Start at 12 o'clock with the curry paste, followed by the halved lemon grass, lime leaves, toasted coconut, the spice-coated beef and lastly the stock.

6. Heat a large saucepan to a medium heat, add the paste and fry for 5–6 minutes until fragrant and deeper in colour. Add the lemon grass and lime leaves and the toasted coconut and fry for 1–2 minutes. Then add the beef and stir well, coating each piece of meat with the flavourful paste. Pour in the stock and bring to a boil, then reduce the heat to low and simmer gently for 3–5 hours, or until the sauce is reduced by half, stirring and scraping the sauce from the bottom of the pan every 15–20 minutes. You are aiming for a thick curry sauce that coats the meat. Once the meat is a melt-in-the-mouth texture and the desired consistency of the sauce is reached, serve garnished with chopped coriander.

4 whole chicken legs
(thigh and drumstick),
with skin and bone
1 lemon grass stalk, trimmed,
bruised and finely chopped
5 lime leaves
1 tomato, diced
generous handful of lemon
basil or basil leaves
vegetable oil

MARINADE
1 tablespoon grated lime
zest and juice of 1 lime
1 teaspoon salt

CHILLI PASTE
6–8 large red chillies
4–5 large green chillies
1 thumb-sized piece
of ginger, peeled
4–5 garlic cloves, peeled
1 teaspoon salt

CHILLI CHILLI CHICKEN

There's a lot of chilli in this recipe, as its title indicates, translated from the Indonesian *ayam rica rica*, but adding salt to the large red chillies when frying them helps to bring out their natural sweetness and control and balance out the flavours, preventing the dish from being over-spicy. If you want to tone down the chilli, you absolutely can, but the beauty of this dish is how the chilli and tomatoes marry in flavour and bring a punch of spice and colour to the feasting table.

1. Mix the marinade ingredients together then massage the marinade into the chicken legs and set aside in a bowl.

2. Roughly chop the chilli paste ingredients or chop and then pulse them in a food processor to form a coarse paste.

3. **Build Your Wok Clock:** Start at 12 o'clock with the marinated chicken, followed by the lemon grass, lime leaves, chilli paste, the tomato and lastly the lemon basil or basil leaves.

4. Heat 1 tablespoon of vegetable oil in a thick-based pan or wok on a medium-high heat until smoking hot. Place the chicken pieces in the pan and sear them for 3–4 minutes until golden brown on the underside, then flip them over to sear the other side. Once browned all over, remove the chicken and set aside.

5. Heat another 2 tablespoons of vegetable oil in the pan to a medium heat, add the lemon grass and lime leaves followed immediately by the chilli paste and stir-fry for 5–6 minutes. Add the tomato and bring the mixture to a vigorous boil before reducing the heat to low.

6. Return the chicken to the pan and simmer for 20–25 minutes, folding the sauce into the chicken every few minutes while it cooks through. Just before serving, scatter the lemon basil or basil leaves over the chicken, fold through and serve.

AROMATIC MEATBALLS

2–3 heads of pak choi
1–2 tablespoons ready-made
   crispy fried onions or shallots,
   to serve

MEATBALLS
200g (7oz) minced beef
200g (7oz) minced chicken
3–4 Thai shallots (swapsies:
   1 brown shallot),
   finely chopped
2 tablespoons cornflour
1 teaspoon salt
½ teaspoon white pepper
1 egg, lightly beaten

CHICKEN SOUP
2 litres (3½ pints) chicken stock
1 tablespoon kecap manis
   (sweet soy sauce)
1 tablespoon oyster sauce
1 thumb-sized piece of ginger,
   peeled and sliced
4 shallots, halved
6 garlic cloves, peeled and
   kept whole

With a large Muslim community in Indonesia, the go-to meats are beef, chicken or lamb rather than pork. In this dish, known as *bakso*, you often find a combination of meats, as you would in the Spanish equivalent *albondigas*, and I've gone for minced beef and chicken, but you can use whichever minced meat you prefer. It can also be served as a noodle soup, a great option if you're cooking this as a stand-alone dish. Just pour the hot soup over cooked or blanched fresh noodles to enjoy as a simple lunch or dinner. However, in the context of a feast, it makes the perfect accompaniment to some rice and deeper-flavoured curries.

1. Mix the meatball ingredients together thoroughly in a mixing bowl by beating vigorously with a wooden spoon, or pound the mixture to a uniform paste by cupping one hand, picking up the mixture and throwing it back into the mixing bowl. Repeating this 5–10 times helps to tenderize the meat and knock out any air pockets in the paste. You can also use an electric mixer fitted with a flat beater (paddle) attachment, and beat the mixture on a low-medium speed for 2 minutes.

2. Place a bowl of cold water nearby for wetting your hands at regular intervals, then form the meatball mixture into table tennis-sized balls. Set aside.

3. Place all the chicken soup ingredients in a large saucepan and bring to a boil on a high heat. Then reduce the heat to medium-low and simmer for at least 20 minutes.

4. When you are ready to serve, bring the chicken soup back to a medium heat, add the meatballs and cook for 4–5 minutes until they are cooked through and floating on the top of the soup. Add the pak choi and cook for a minute. Top with the crispy onions or shallots and serve.

I
N
D
O
N
E
S
I
A
N

STIR-FRIED PICKLED VEGETABLES

Acar kuning is a traditional side dish that is found on almost every menu in Indonesia, and is often used as a colourful topping for fish and meats too. The vegetables are fried in a sweet, sour and salty sauce, which reminds me of a time when my wife accidently cooked our Chinese greens at home with rice vinegar instead of rice wine and I scoffed at her for doing so. Turns out the joke was on me – they were delicious! As in all cases, however, if you add a bit of sugar and salt to the vinegar, suddenly the pure sourness becomes balanced and palatable. And yes, I've already thanked my wife for recipe testing for me years in advance without even knowing it!

4-5 Thai shallots, peeled
  and kept whole (swapsies:
  1 red onion, quartered)
3-5 birds' eye chillies, pierced
  with the tip of your knife
2-3 carrots, halved and sliced
  lengthways into eighths
½ cucumber, cut into
  4cm (1½ inch) batons
vegetable oil

SPICE PASTE
6-7 Thai shallots (swapsies:
  1 large red onion),
  finely chopped
3 garlic cloves, finely chopped
1 teaspoon ground turmeric

PICKLING SAUCE
3-4 tablespoons rice vinegar
3-4 tablespoons water
½ teaspoon sugar
¼ teaspoon salt

1. Pound the spice paste ingredients together using a pestle and mortar, adding them one at a time, or blitz them in a food processor to form a smooth paste (you may need a tablespoon of water if using a machine).

2. Mix the pickling sauce ingredients together in a small bowl.

3. **Build Your Wok Clock:** Start at 12 o'clock with the spice paste, followed by the whole Thai shallots, chillies, carrots, cucumbers and lastly the pickling sauce.

4. Heat 1 tablespoon of vegetable oil in a wok to a medium heat. Add the spice paste and stir-fry for 1-2 minutes. Then add the Thai shallots and chillies, stir-frying for 15-20 seconds after each addition. Add the carrots and stir-fry for 3-4 minutes until softened and to combine the flavours, then add the cucumbers and stir-fry for 30-60 seconds.

5. Increase the heat to high, pour in the pickling sauce and bring to a vigorous boil for 30-60 seconds. Tip into a bowl and serve.

INDONESIAN

AROMATIC COCONUT RICE

In Indonesia, as in many Asian cultures, rice is life. It also signifies fertility and wealth, so an Indonesian feast is nothing without it. When cooked with fresh spices and aromatics as in this dish (*nasi liwet*), I could easily eat it on its own simply with some homemade sambal on the side (see page 122).

1. Wash the rice at least 3 times, if not 5–6 times (in Chinese tradition, we don't do things by 4s, as it's unlucky!). Place the rice in a bowl and run under cold water, gently moving the rice grains between the tips of your fingers. The excess starch from the rice grains will initially make the water quite cloudy, so pour the rice through a sieve in between each wash. Repeat until the water runs clear. Sieve one last time and set aside.

2. Heat 2 tablespoons of vegetable oil in a saucepan to a medium heat, add the dried anchovies or crispy onions or shallots and fry for 30–60 seconds until crisp and golden brown. Then remove from the oil using a slotted spoon, reserving the oil in the pan.

3. Mix the stock ingredients together in a jug.

4. **Build Your Wok Clock:** Start at 12 o'clock with the shallots, followed by the garlic, chillies, lime leaves, bay leaves, lemon grass, the rice, the stock and lastly the fried dried anchovies or crispy onions or shallots.

5. Reheat the now flavourful oil to a medium heat, add the shallots and garlic and stir-fry for 30 seconds. Continue working around the wok clock up until the rice, adding each ingredient in turn and stir-frying for 30 seconds after each addition. Then add the rice and stir through the flavoured oil for 30–60 seconds. Pour in the stock and add half the fried anchovies or crispy onions or shallots. Cover with a tight-fitting lid, increase the heat to medium-high heat and bring to a vigorous boil. Then reduce the heat to low and simmer with the lid on for 12–15 minutes until the liquid has evaporated to the point where you start to see air pockets form in between some of the rice grains. Replace the lid, turn the heat off and leave the rice to sit for another 15 minutes. Fluff up with a fork, then garnish with the rest of the fried anchovies or crispy onions or shallots and serve.

2 cups of jasmine, basmati
    or white long-grain rice
    (I use a 240ml/8½fl oz cup,
    holding 195g/7oz rice)
handful of dried anchovies
    (*ikan bilis*) or ready-made
    crispy fried onions or shallots
3–4 Thai shallots (swapsies:
    ½ banana shallot),
    finely sliced
3–4 garlic cloves,
    roughly chopped
3–4 birds' eye chillies,
    kept whole
5–6 lime leaves
3–4 bay leaves
2 lemon grass stalks,
    trimmed, bruised
    and halved lengthways
vegetable oil

STOCK
1½ cups (see above)
    of coconut milk
1½ cups (see above) of chicken
    or vegetable stock
½ teaspoon sugar
¼ teaspoon salt

BANANA LEAF ROASTED FISH

½ tablespoon palm sugar
(swapsies: soft brown sugar)
1 teaspoon salt
2 x 300g (10½oz) firm white
fish fillets (such as cod, hake,
halibut or pollock), with skin
1–2 banana leaves (swapsies:
baking paper)
vegetable oil

SAMBAL
4–5 large red chillies,
finely chopped
3–4 garlic cloves, finely chopped
2 lemon grass stalks, trimmed,
bruised and finely chopped
1 thumb-sized piece
of galangal or ginger,
peeled and finely chopped
1 teaspoon ground turmeric
½ handful of macadamia nuts
or blanched hazelnuts,
finely chopped

I've cooked this dish, called *ikan pepes* in Indonesian, the traditional way here using banana leaves, but if you can't find any near you, you can always use baking paper instead for ease. You can also cook the parcel directly over a barbecue if you want more of a smoky, steamed finish to the fish. The sambal recipe will make enough to flavour the dish, but if your family are like mine, double or triple the quantities and save the remainder in a jar for the rest of the family feast or to enjoy with breakfast, lunch and dinner the next day!

1. Pound the sambal ingredients together using a pestle and mortar, adding them one at a time, or blitz them in a food processor to form a smooth paste (you may need to add a tablespoon or so of water if using a machine).

2. Heat 2–3 tablespoons of vegetable oil in a frying pan or wok to a medium heat, add the sambal paste and fry for 5–6 minutes, stirring every minute or so, until it turns deeper in colour. Add the palm sugar and salt and continue to fry until the paste is fragrant and dark reddish-brown.

3. Make 3–4 diagonal slits across the skin of the fish fillets and lay the fish on the banana leaf or sheet of baking paper. Massage 3–4 tablespoons of the sambal into the fish fillets, setting aside any remaining sambal for dipping. Wrap the fish up in the banana leaf or baking paper to make a parcel and 'sew' it closed by roughly weaving a bamboo skewer through the top. Place the parcel in a roasting tray.

4. Preheat the oven to 220°C/475°F/Gas Mark 9. Bake the fish for 15–20 minutes, depending on the thickness of your fillet. Open the parcel to serve.

I
N
D
O
N
E
S
I
A
N

SWEETCORN & CHIVE FRITTERS

1 teaspoon coriander seeds
3 sweetcorn cobs, kernels
  cut off the cobs
handful of Chinese chives
  (flowering, if possible)
  (swapsies: chives), chopped
  into 5mm (¼ inch) pieces
3 spring onions, sliced
3 garlic cloves, finely chopped
½ green chilli, finely chopped
1 teaspoon salt
½ teaspoon ground turmeric
vegetable oil

BATTER
1 egg, lightly beaten
60g (2¼oz) plain flour
20g (¾oz) cornflour

I love the way Lara Lee describes the textural experience of eating something fried and crunchy and explains how important it is in providing balance in an Indonesian feast. While you can shallow-fry these corn fritters (*perkedel jagung*) in a large pan, which is what I would do if cooking them for a midweek family meal, my preference, especially when cooking for a feast, is to deep-fry them, as I love the extra CRUNCH you get from the individual corn kernels. So satisfying! The sambal on page 122 makes the perfect accompaniment.

1. Pound the coriander seeds using a pestle and mortar to form a coarse powder. Add half the sweetcorn kernels and gently crush them into a rough sweetcorn mash. (This mash mixes well with the batter and helps the mixture hold its shape.)

2. Transfer the sweetcorn mash to a mixing bowl, add the rest of the sweetcorn kernels along with the other ingredients (except the batter) and mix well. Finally, add the batter ingredients to the bowl and massage the mixture together with your hands until just combined.

3. Half-fill a wok or deep-fryer with vegetable oil and bring to a medium-high heat. Test the temperature of the oil by placing the tip of a wooden chopstick or skewer in the oil. If it starts to fizz after a second or so, the oil has reached the desired temperature of around 180°C/350°F.

4. Carefully lay 1 large heaped tablespoon of the fritter mixture in the oil. Continue to lay the mixture in the oil, spoon by spoon, taking care not to overfill your wok or fryer, as each fritter needs enough space to float and fry without sticking to another. Fry for 2–3 minutes until golden brown on the underside, then turn over and fry the other side until golden brown. Remove with a slotted spoon and place on a plate lined with kitchen paper to drain the excess oil before serving. Fry the fritters in batches if necessary to avoid overcrowding.

CHIPS & GADO GADO

My friend Jaideep obsesses about the Curacao food trucks that slather chips in peanut sauce. This is my take on amalgamated Caribbean, Dutch and Indonesian influences, that combines three of the best things in life: salad, peanut sauce and chips.

1. Blanch the beans in a saucepan of boiling water for 3 minutes, remove with a slotted spoon and cool in cold water. Blanch the spinach, then the beansprouts, separately for 30 seconds. Place in separate bowls of cold water. Drain them all.

2. Boil the eggs in a saucepan of boiling water for 6½ minutes. Drain and allow to cool, then peel and halve.

3. Massage the salt into the chips and leave them to sit in a bowl for 5–10 minutes. Pat dry with a clean tea towel.

4. Pound the spice paste ingredients together using a pestle and mortar, adding them one at a time, or blitz them in a food processor to form a smooth paste (you may need a tablespoon of water). Mix the sauce ingredients, except the peanut butter, in a jug, then stir in the peanut butter until well combined.

5. **Build Your Wok Clock:** Start at 12 o'clock with the spice paste, followed by the sauce, chips, salad ingredients and egg halves.

6. Heat 2 tablespoons of vegetable oil in a saucepan to a medium heat, stir in the paste and fry for 4–5 minutes until deeper in colour. Pour over the sauce and bring to a boil, then reduce the heat to low and simmer for 10–15 minutes, stirring occasionally.

7. Meanwhile, half-fill a wok or deep-fryer with vegetable oil and bring to a medium heat. Test the temperature by placing the tip of a wooden chopstick into the oil. If it gently bubbles rather than quickly fizzing, the temperature is right. Carefully lay the chips in the oil and fry for 5 minutes, or until lightly golden and cooked through. Remove with a slotted spoon. Bring the oil up up to a medium-high heat, so your chopstick starts to fizz after a second or so. Fry the chips for another 1–2 minutes to a deeper golden brown. Remove and drain on 2 sheets of kitchen paper.

8. Assemble your salad, then add the chips and eggs on top, with the sauce served on the side, garnished with the red chilli.

75g (2½oz) green beans
large handful of Chinese
    or baby spinach
150g (5½oz) beansprouts, rinsed
2–3 eggs
¼ teaspoon salt
1 large potato, unpeeled, cut
    into 5mm (¼ inch) thick chips
½ cucumber, in bite-sized wedges
2 tomatoes, in bite-sized wedges
vegetable oil
1 red chilli, deseeded and finely
    sliced into rings, to garnish

GADO GADO SPICE PASTE
4–5 Thai shallots (swapsies:
    1 red onion), finely chopped
4–5 large red chillies,
    finely chopped
3–4 garlic cloves, finely chopped
2 lemon grass stalks, trimmed,
    bruised and finely chopped
1 thumb-sized piece of ginger,
    peeled and finely chopped

GADO GADO SAUCE
400ml (14fl oz) coconut milk
150ml (5fl oz) water
4 tablespoons kecap manis
    (sweet soy sauce)
2 tablespoons tamarind
    concentrate or juice of ¼ lime
1 teaspoon salt
6 tablespoons smooth
    peanut butter

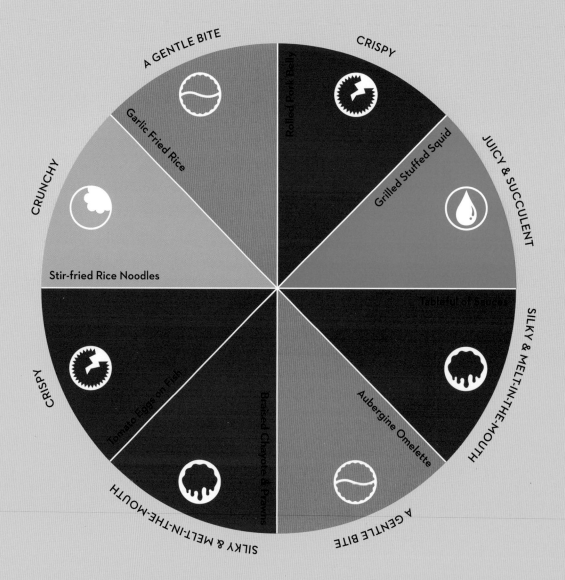

A GENTLE BITE

CRISPY

Rolled Pork Belly

Grilled Stuffed Squid

JUICY & SUCCULENT

Garlic Fried Rice

CRUNCHY

Stir-fried Rice Noodles

Tableful of Sauces

SILKY & MELT-IN-THE-MOUTH

CRISPY

Tomato Eggs on Fish

Aubergine Omelette

Braised Chayote & Prawns

SILKY & MELT-IN-THE-MOUTH

A GENTLE BITE

PINOY

I love that one word — *kamayan* — can describe the Filipino tradition of 'eating a feast with hands' in such a simple way. Imagine long communal tables on a beach or under a bamboo hut, layered with strips of banana leaf, topped with piles of food. Each mound of garlic rice (see page 144), fried fish (see page 142) or slow-roasted pork is carefully placed on patches of the leaves to ensure everyone at the table can sit within arm's reach of every dish. It's a feasting sensation that takes sharing food to the next level: a feast for the eyes, a feast with your hands and a true feast for the heart. As with many of the South East Asian cultures, the etiquette around eating here is to dig in, and to do so with gusto in a totally informal way. If there's something saucy in the feast, get a spoon of it over to your plate or your own sheet of banana leaf and mop it up with the rice or meat.

In recent years, Pinoy cuisine has become famous through chains that churn out their version of Filipino fried chicken and super-sweet spaghetti in tomato sauce. Unfortunately, like any chain, I don't think places like this do justice to the prowess that Pinoy food has to offer. My hope is that my small version of a *kamayan* feast here inspires you to explore the real cuisine in a little more depth. It has numerous types of roasted pig, from *lechon liempo* (see page 134) to *lechon de leche* (roast suckling pig), exhibiting the obvious influence of the Spanish *cochinillo*. Notable too are beautifully braised squash or pumpkin dishes and grilled fish and seafood (an archipelago essential), all rounded off with the true Filipino power – piles and piles of rice – accompanied by sauces and pickles (see page 146) to slather over it all.

With 7,640 islands making up the Philippines, it's near impossible to put together a list of dishes that represent all Pinoy cuisines, but there are certainly some standout favourites that everyone should know

(*Adobo* is one, a recipe for which you can find in my previous School of Wok book *Delicious Asian Food in Minutes*). The dishes in this chapter have been hand-picked with the intention of encouraging you to find some banana leaf from an Asian store, get creative and change your way of eating forever. Need further inspiration? Flick ahead to the sample feast on pages 148-9 and you'll know it will be worth the effort.

In true Pinoy style, go low and slow with the Rolled Pork Belly and get started early on with this showstopper. Squid has quite a tough membrane that also takes time to marinate, so get the Grilled Stuffed Squid prepared well in advance ready to grill it for 10 minutes before serving the whole meal. If you're the kind of host who won't let your guests do any work when they arrive, then get the Tableful of Sauces ready beforehand for their flavours to develop over time. Personally, I like to put my guests to work, and chopping and shaking together some simple sauces is a great way for them to help on their arrival and to have some company in the kitchen. It's the aubergine for the Aubergine Omelette that takes time to cook, while you will want to cook the omelette fresh, so prepare everything in advance to make the dish easy to finish off later – the aubergine will warm through once cooked coated in the beaten egg mixture just before serving. Likewise, it's the chayote for the Braised Chayote & Prawns that takes a while, so if preparing it as part of a bigger feast, I'd suggest cooking the dish up until the stage where the prawns are added, then reheating and finishing it 5 minutes before serving after popping in the prawns. The Tomato Eggs on Fish is quick and easy to cook, so you can prep this early but cook it at the last minute for freshness. Then I'd recommend either the Stir-fried Rice Noodles or Garlic Fried Rice, both of which can be prepped and cooked towards the very end of your feast preparations.

ROLLED PORK BELLY

2–2.5kg (4lb 8oz–5lb 8oz)
    boneless pork belly,
    with skin
2–3 teaspoons salt

MARINADE
3–4 garlic cloves, finely chopped
1 tablespoon onion powder
1½ teaspoons sea salt
1½ teaspoons black pepper
1 teaspoon sugar
1 tablespoon rice vinegar
    or white wine vinegar
1 tablespoon vegetable oil

STUFFING
1 large red onion, finely sliced
5 spring onions, roughly
    chopped
5–6 garlic cloves, roughly
    chopped
3 lemon grass stalks, trimmed
    and well bruised

DIPPING SAUCE
150ml (5fl oz) rice vinegar
    or white wine vinegar
½ teaspoon salt
½ teaspoon black pepper
3 Thai shallots (swapsies:
    ½ red onion), finely sliced
2–3 mixed chillies,
    roughly chopped
1 spring onion, finely chopped
¼ cucumber, diced
2 tablespoons palm sugar
    (swapsies: soft brown sugar)

I have vivid memories of the bus 'system' in Palawan, an island south of Manila, where the bus stops in random and remote places. There was always a familiarity and comfort from the alluring aroma of slowly sizzling pork fat nearby, whether from a whole suckling pig or a rolled slab of pork belly (*lechon liempo*). Given my family's predilection for all things pork and the prevalence of it in Palawan, its mouth-watering scent worked to endear the island, and even its public transport, to me.

1. Score vertically across the skin of the pork belly every 5mm (¼ inch), cutting through part of the fat but not into the meat, to help the salt penetrate the skin and crisp up when roasting.

2. Turn the pork belly skin-side down and score the meat diagonally about 5mm (¼ inch) deep all the way across at 2cm (¾ inch) intervals. Mix the marinade ingredients together, then rub over the flesh (not the skin). Scatter the stuffing ingredients across the meat with the lemon grass stalks in the centre. Cut 8 pieces of butcher's twine, long enough to wrap around the rolled belly. Space them evenly under the skin, roll up the belly and tie, allowing a bit of slack for the skin to crackle and expand.

3. Preheat the oven to 130°C/300°F/Gas Mark 2. Blanch the rolled belly in a large saucepan of boiling water for 4–5 minutes. Carefully remove with tongs, then pat the skin completely dry with kitchen paper. Rub the skin with the salt and leave to sit for 10 minutes, then again, pat the skin dry with kitchen paper. Place the rolled belly on a wire rack set over a roasting tray and roast for 2–2½ hours until cooked through.

4. Meanwhile, place all the sauce ingredients in a saucepan, bring to a boil and stir until the sugar has dissolved and set aside.

5. Increase the oven temperature to 210°C/450°F/Gas Mark 8. If it's possible to turn off the fan in your oven, do so and increase the temperature by 20°C. Roast the pork for another 15–20 minutes until crackling has formed around the whole roll – once the top has crackled, you may need to turn the pork every 5–10 minutes to crisp up each side. Remove and leave to rest for 10–15 minutes. Slice into thick pieces and serve with the dipping sauce.

10 large raw peeled
    tiger prawns
½ thumb-sized piece of ginger,
    peeled and roughly chopped
3 garlic cloves, roughly chopped
2 chayote, about 600–800g
    (1lb 5oz–1lb 12oz) (swapsies:
    1 marrow or other
    summer squash), cut into
    bite-sized chunks
½ teaspoon chilli flakes
5–6 cherry tomatoes, halved
vegetable oil

SAUCE
200ml (7fl oz) chicken stock
1 tablespoon oyster sauce
½ teaspoon salt
¼ teaspoon black pepper

BRAISED CHAYOTE & PRAWNS

Members of the squash family are pretty easy to grow
and if left to their own devices just seem to keep on growing
or multiplying, and with their sturdy skins they are hard
to damage. Walk through any market in the Philippines,
or in fact most South East Asian or Chinese cities, and you'll
stumble across many different varieties of squash, like the
bumpy green chayote (or sayote) gourd, and you may well
be at a loss as to what to do with them. Here's a super-simple
recipe that works a treat with most squash, wherever you
live. Eat with a bowl of steamed rice or fried noodles on
the side.

1. Butterfly the prawns by running a knife down the backs
through the meat to open them out, then rinse them under
cold running water to remove the black digestive cord.

2. Mix the sauce ingredients together in a jug.

3. **Build Your Wok Clock:** Start at 12 o'clock with the ginger and
garlic, followed by the chayote, chilli flakes, the sauce, tomatoes
and lastly the prawns.

4. Heat 1 tablespoon of vegetable oil in a wok to a medium heat,
add the ginger and garlic and stir-fry for 1 minute until golden
brown. Increase the heat to high, add the chayote and stir-fry
for 3–4 minutes, then add the chilli flakes and stir-fry for another
2–3 minutes. Pour in half the sauce and bring to a vigorous boil.
Stir, then cover with a lid, reduce the heat to medium heat and
cook for 10–15 minutes until the chayote is tender.

5. Remove the lid, return the heat to high and add the tomatoes,
then pour in the rest of the sauce and boil for 5 minutes. Add the
prawns and cook for about 3–4 minutes until they have turned
coral pink in colour, then serve.

AUBERGINE OMELETTE

4 aubergines
2 eggs
2 garlic cloves, finely chopped
vegetable oil
¼ teaspoon black pepper
salt
Sawsawan (see page 146),
    to serve

Like me, Filipinos adore eggs, for breakfast, lunch or dinner cooked in numerous different ways. I have fond memories of camping out in bamboo huts overlooking pristine waters in the remote islands in the Philippines and recall waking up and catching one of the local chefs strolling past us with a massive grin on his face, serving up an omelette stuffed with a whole aubergine. He wore the expression of supreme satisfaction that comes from a chef who knows just from looking at his simple creation how good it's going to taste. Since there's no better reason to feel smug, I've included this recipe so that you can too! Why not close your eyes and imagine you're on a white sandy beach while you're eating it.

1. Preheat the oven to 210°C/450°F/Gas Mark 8. Rub 1 tablespoon of vegetable oil and ½ a teaspoon of salt all over the aubergines. Place them in a roasting tray and roast for 30–35 minutes.

2. Meanwhile, beat the eggs together in a mixing bowl, then season with the garlic, pepper and ½ teaspoon salt and mix well.

3. Once the aubergines are cooked through, they will look and feel soft with the skin slightly wrinkled and you will be able to push a fork or knife straight through without any resistance. If there is still some resistance, return to the oven for another 5 minutes and check again. Remove the aubergines from the oven and allow them to cool slightly, then peel, taking care to keep the flesh of the aubergines intact and attached to the stem. Lightly press the flesh of each aubergine down onto a plate with a fork to fan out slightly, shaping it into a flat pear shape.

4. Heat 2–3 tablespoons of vegetable oil in a large frying pan (about 40cm/16 inches, which should fit 2 of the flattened aubergines) to a medium-high heat. Dip 2 of the aubergines in turn into the beaten egg mixture so that they are well covered, place in the hot oil and fry for about 3–4 minutes until golden brown on the underside. Flip them over and fry on the other side until golden brown. Transfer to a plate lined with kitchen paper to drain the excess oil. Repeat with the remaining 2 aubergines. Serve with any of the sauces (*Sawsawan*) on page 46 on the side.

GRILLED STUFFED SQUID

4 large squid, cleaned,
   tentacles separated
   and bodies kept whole
vegetable oil

FILLING
4 tomatoes, finely chopped
2 red onions, finely chopped
1 thumb-sized piece of ginger,
   peeled and finely chopped
2 tablespoons fish sauce

MARINADE
100ml (3½fl oz) lemonade
   (traditionally the fizzy kind,
   but any type will work)
3 tablespoons light soy sauce
2 tablespoons fish sauce
juice of ½ lime
1 tablespoon palm sugar
   (swapsies: soft brown sugar)
½ teaspoon cracked
   black pepper

TO SERVE
Sawsawan (see page 146)
lime wedges

Keeping with the sweet–savoury song sheet, here's another simple dish that can be prepared ahead of time and then quickly grilled or pan-fried just before serving. As long as the marinade has had time to soak into the squid, you'll get a lovely caramelized finish on the outside of the seafood when grilling. Notice the use of lemonade, again illustrating the sweeter nature of Pinoy cuisine.

1. Mix the filling ingredients together, then stuff each of the squid bodies until three-quarters full with the mixture. Place in a bowl with the tentacles.

2. Mix the marinade ingredients together in a jug, then pour over the squid bodies and tentacles and massage well into the squid. 'Sew' the opening of each stuffed squid body closed by weaving a bamboo skewer through the top. The legs can be kept separate or woven onto the skewers along with the bodies. Return the squid to the marinade, cover and refrigerate for at least 2 hours, preferably overnight.

3. Heat a griddle pan, frying pan or barbecue to a high heat. Brush the squid with a little vegetable oil, place them directly on the hot pan or barbecue and sear for 2–3 minutes, then flip over and sear the other side. Remove and slice into 1cm (½ inch) thick rings. Serve with any of the sauces (*Sawsawan*) on page 146 and some lime wedges on the side for squeezing over.

2 sea bream fillets, with skin, descaled
1 red onion, cut into wedges
2 spring onions, roughly chopped, plus 1, finely sliced, to garnish
2 tomatoes, cut into wedges
vegetable oil

EGG MIXTURE
2 eggs
¼ teaspoon salt
¼ teaspoon white pepper

SAUCE
50ml (2fl oz) chicken or vegetable stock
2 tablespoons tomato ketchup
1 tablespoon fish sauce
1 tablespoon sugar

TOMATO EGGS ON FISH

This recipe, known as Fish *Sarciado*, brings together two of my favourite ingredients, fish and eggs, in an unusual but delicious way. The combination of sweet, savoury and slightly sour flavours in the sauce is highly characteristic of Pinoy cuisine. I have put my own stamp on this dish by topping the pan-fried fish with a Chinese-style tomato egg stir-fry. So moreish, I'd happily serve this as a one-pan wonder for a midweek meal.

1. Beat the eggs together in a mixing bowl, then season with the salt and pepper and mix well.

2. Mix the sauce ingredients together in a jug.

3. **Build Your Wok Clock:** Start at 12 o'clock with the fish fillets, followed by the egg mixture, red onion, roughly chopped spring onions, tomatoes and lastly the sauce.

4. Heat 2–3 tablespoons of vegetable oil in a large frying pan to a high heat. Dab the skin of the fish fillets dry with kitchen paper, then carefully place them skin-side down in the pan and fry for 1 minute, pressing down on the fillets with a spatula to crisp up the skin. Then reduce the heat to medium-low and fry for 4–5 minutes, pressing down on the fish to sear them well. Carefully flip the fillets over and fry for another 1–2 minutes. Transfer them to a serving plate.

5. Heat 2 tablespoons of vegetable oil in a wok to a high heat until smoking hot. Pour in the egg mixture and swirl it around the wok, then start to fold the egg into the wok and stir-fry for 1–2 minutes until half-cooked. Tip the mixture onto a plate. Add ½ tablespoon of vegetable oil to the wok and heat until smoking hot, then add the red onion, roughly chopped spring onions and tomatoes in turn, stir-frying for 30 seconds after each addition. Return the half-cooked egg to the wok, immediately pour in the sauce and bring to a vigorous boil. Fold the sauce through the ingredients until well mixed, then pour over the fried fish, garnish with the finely sliced spring onion and serve.

STIR-FRIED RICE NOODLES

As with many countries all over the world, there has long been a Chinese influence on Pinoy cuisine. Stir-fried noodle dishes are perhaps the most obvious evidence of this, passed from generation to generation with slightly different variations as they are adapted from one cuisine to another. Called *pancit bihon* in Filipino, in the takeaway world I'd call this a 'special fried noodle' dish, as it's packed with two types of meat and loads of different vegetables, along with a mix of Chinese sauces and a touch of Spanish in the form of the paprika. Essentially, put whatever you want into it, follow the wok clock and you'll be just fine.

300g (10½oz) rice vermicelli
150g (5½oz) pork
    shoulder steaks
150g (5½oz) skinless,
    boneless chicken thighs
½ onion, finely sliced
1 carrot, cut into matchsticks
100g (3½oz) sugarsnaps,
    halved lengthways
2 sweetheart cabbage leaves,
    finely shredded
vegetabe oil
½ lime, cut into wedges,
    to garnish

SAUCE
50ml (2fl oz) chicken stock
2 tablespoons light soy sauce
½ tablespoon oyster sauce
½ tablespoon dark soy sauce
4 garlic cloves, finely chopped
1 teaspoon paprika
½ teaspoon sugar

1. Soak the vermicelli in hot water for 3 minutes until the noodles have separated, then drain and refresh in cold water. Drain again and spread out on a clean tea towel to dry for 10 minutes.

2. Mix the sauce ingredients together in a jug.

3. Fill a saucepan three-quarters full with hot water and bring to a boil on a medium-high heat. Add the pork steaks and chicken thighs and boil for 15 minutes, then drain and finely slice into thin shreds of meat.

4. **Build Your Wok Clock:** Start at 12 o'clock with the shredded pork and chicken, followed by the onion, carrot, sugarsnaps, noodles, the sauce and lastly the cabbage.

5. Heat 1 tablespoon of vegetable oil in a wok on a high heat until smoking, add the shredded meat and stir-fry for 2–3 minutes until it is starting to brown. Then add the onion, carrot and sugarsnaps in turn, stir-frying for 30 seconds after each addition. Add the noodles and stir-fry for 2–3 minutes, then stop stirring for at least 30 seconds to allow the wok to come up to a high heat. Pour in the sauce and bring to a vigorous boil, then stir-fry for a minute or so. Just before serving, add the cabbage and fold through until wilted but still keeping its crunch. Serve with the lime wedges on the side to garnish.

GARLIC FRIED RICE

10 garlic cloves, finely chopped
2 spring onions, finely chopped
550g (1lb 4oz) cooked white
    rice, at room temperature
vegetable oil
¼ teaspoon sea salt
¼ teaspoon black pepper

Across the Philippines, rice is known as Filipino power, so this rice dish should be regarded as souped-up Filipino power that will go with any of the meals in this whole book. This is such a simple way to flavour an average bowl of steamed white rice, but just be careful not to burn the garlic, as it will change colour quite quickly!

1. Heat 2 tablespoons of vegetable oil in a wok to a medium heat and add the garlic, then gently swirl the oil around, fold the garlic through and stir-fry it for 2–3 minutes until it all turns evenly light golden brown in colour. Immediately pour the oil and garlic through a sieve set over a bowl and allow the excess oil to drain from the garlic.

2. Set aside the fried garlic and reheat the garlic oil in the wok on a medium-high heat until smoking hot. Add the spring onions, quickly followed by the cooked rice and stir-fry for 3–4 minutes until the grains have separated and are piping hot all the way through. Season with the salt and pepper, top the with the fried garlic and serve.

TABLEFUL OF SAUCES

Sawsawan, meaning side sauces and condiments, are a huge part of Pinoy cuisine and are often brought separately to the table, to allow everyone to make up their own concoction of condiments during a family feast. Homemade vinegar and calamansi lime-based sauces can often be found sitting in jars, ready to mix with soy sauce to help cut through the richness of barbecued meats and grilled fish or seafood. Here are a few sauces that would work a treat with any of the rice, noodles or grilled dishes both in this chapter and throughout the book. All of them will keep in the fridge in a sterilized airtight jar for up to a week.

TOYOMANSI

PREP: 5 MINS
SERVES/MAKES 100ML (3½FL OZ)

3 large red chillies, finely chopped
juice of 6 calamansi limes (swapsies: 1 lime and 1 mandarin)
4 tablespoons light soy sauce
2 tablespoons fish sauce

Mix all the ingredients together in a bowl and serve.

SINAMAK

PREP: 10 MINS, PLUS INFUSING
MAKES A 250ML (9FL OZ) JAR

10 birds' eye chillies, pierced with the tip of your knife
6 garlic cloves, roughly chopped
3 Thai shallots, finely sliced (swapsies: ½ red onion)
2 thumb-sized pieces of galangal, peeled and cut into matchsticks (swapsies: ginger)
150ml (5fl oz) coconut vinegar (swapsies: rice vinegar)

Mix all the ingredients together in a sterilized airtight jar, seal and refrigerate for 1–2 days to allow the flavours to infuse into the vinegar.

SOUR CHILLI SAUCE

PREP: 10 MINS, PLUS INFUSING
COOK: 5 MINS
MAKES A 250ML (9FL OZ) JAR

10 large red chillies, pierced with the tip of your knife
½ red pepper, peeled, cored and roughly chopped
2 garlic cloves, roughly chopped
1 teaspoon salt
½ teaspoon black peppercorns
¼ teaspoon sugar
150ml (5fl oz) coconut vinegar (swapsies: rice vinegar)

Place all the ingredients in a saucepan and bring to a vigorous boil for 1 minute. Transfer to a food processor and blitz until smooth. Then pour into a sterilized airtight jar and leave to cool. Seal and refrigerate for 1–2 days to allow the flavours to infuse into the vinegar, then serve.

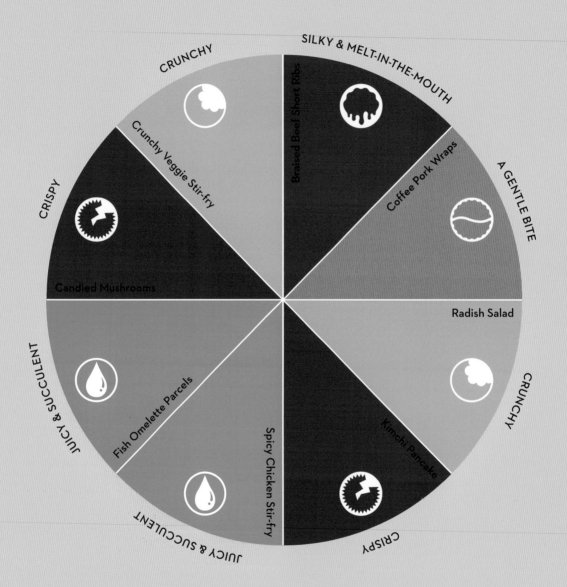

CRUNCHY

SILKY & MELT-IN-THE-MOUTH

Braised Beef Short Ribs

Crunchy Veggie Stir-fry

CRISPY

Coffee Pork Wraps

A GENTLE BITE

Candied Mushrooms

Radish Salad

JUICY & SUCCULENT

CRUNCHY

Fish Omelette Parcels

Kimchi Pancake

Spicy Chicken Stir-fry

JUICY & SUCCULENT

CRISPY

KOREAN

I often think about lunchtimes at the Korean technology firm where I worked way before starting my culinary career. The lunch hall was comprised of two canteens: the cafe (essentially a sandwich bar with a soup option), which was, let's put it this way, customer scarce, and a Korean canteen, which had long queues forming daily from 11am. What I loved about the Korean canteen were the steel trays each with four or five segments to contain every part of your meal separately, alongside thin metal bowls filled with steaming hot rice. When eating, there was a sense of rhythm, moving the heavy chopsticks from one part of the tray to another, picking up a bit of kimchi, then over to pick up a clump of rice, pausing for a beat to take it in before heading back over the metal tray into the crispy kimchi pancake (see page 160), noting the crisp and crunch. Then, before moving on to a slow-cooked meaty stew (see page 154), you grab another clump of rice so that you can mop up the silky sauce and melt-in-the-mouth meat in one fell swoop.

Whether in segmented trays or a big bowl of bibimbap in which colourful vegetables are formed in sections around a bowl of rice, Korean eating has a different feeling to Chinese or South East Asian rituals. There is a uniform separation of the components, lending more choice with each bite. Whether you choose to savour every mouthful or scoff it all down, the presentation of all the different elements is what makes it so much fun.

There are clever flavour combinations in Korean food that just hit the spot. The main dishes are usually bold in flavour, combining either sweet, savoury and spicy or spicy, sour and salty, as in that distinct tang you get from kimchi and other pickles. Most meals are balanced out with lots of quickly blanched or stir-fried vegetables, lightly seasoned and kept crisp and fresh, to add that all-important crunch. In my previous School of Wok book, *Delicious Asian Food in Minutes*, I wrote about various vegetable side dishes, or *namul*, which could easily be added to any of these recipes. For simplicity, and to help your Korean home-cooking repertoire, there's a quick mixed *namul*-style veggie stir-fry here to fill the gaps in the table (see page 159).

For your Korean feast, I recommend choosing either the Braised Beef Short Ribs or the Coffee Pork Wraps. You could even cook the ribs for longer than the recipe time, as extra braising will get the bones poking out while still keeping a bite to the meat. Either way, it's worth cooking this dish first. If making the Coffee Pork Wraps instead, these are traditionally served together with the Radish Salad, a great place to start off any Korean meal – keep the salad covered in the fridge until ready to serve. The Kimchi Pancake should be freshly cooked, but it's also hygienically safe to cook it 30 minutes before serving and then either reheat it in the oven preheated to 200°C/425°F/Gas Mark 7 for 5–10 minutes to crisp up the edges or just keep warm and crisp in the oven ready to serve. I would go for the Spicy Chicken Stir-fry next, as the chicken will be moist enough to sit well for a few minutes while you serve up the other dishes. Fish Omelette Parcels are quick and easy to cook, so prep these later on and cook them at the final stage. Deep-frying is best done as a sole task and as close to serving as possible both for safety's sake and the success of your dish, so leave cooking the Candied Mushrooms near to the end. Finally, the Crunchy Veggie Stir-fry is a quick, simple and vibrant balancing act for the meal, so flash-fry it at the last minute. And remember, you can encourage guests to sit down to a few of the slower-cooked dishes, then finish off and serve up the quick-cooks at the end, underlining the notion that it really is a feast with food continually streaming out of the kitchen.

BRAISED BEEF SHORT RIBS

Short rib is a popular cut of meat in Korea and tends to be either grilled Korean barbecue style or slow-cooked as in this recipe using thicker cuts of short rib. The ribs are more pick-upable if you can get your butcher to cut them in half, but alternatively just cook them separated and whole. The sauce creates an incredible sweet and salty glaze over the melt-in-the-mouth meat.

2kg (4lb 8oz) beef short ribs, halved and separated – ask your butcher to chop them
large handful of pine nuts (optional)
½ thumb-sized piece of ginger, peeled and finely chopped
1 head of garlic, cloves separated and finely chopped
5–6 dried shiitake mushrooms, soaked in hot water for at least 2 hours, preferably overnight, then drained and quartered
500ml (18fl oz) chicken stock
3 carrots, cut into large chunks
½ small Korean radish (swapsies: daikon), peeled and cut into large chunks
handful of pitted dried jujube (swapsies: pitted dates)
100g (3½oz) ready-cooked chestnuts
vegetable oil

SAUCE

5 tablespoons light soy sauce
5 tablespoons mirin
3 tablespoons sugar
1 tablespoon maple syrup (swapsies: rice syrup or honey)
½ teaspoon salt

1. Blanch the beef ribs in a large saucepan of boiling water for 5 minutes, then drain and rinse under cold running water to remove any scum or film from the meat.

2. Meanwhile, toast the pine nuts, if using, in a dry frying pan on a medium heat for about 5 minutes until golden brown, then set aside.

3. Mix the sauce ingredients together in a small bowl.

4. **Build Your Wok Clock:** Start at 12 o'clock with the ginger and garlic, followed by the shiitake mushrooms, beef ribs, the sauce, chicken stock, carrots, radish, jujube, chestnuts and lastly the toasted pine nuts, if using.

5. Heat 2 tablespoons of vegetable oil in a large saucepan to a medium heat. Add the ginger and garlic and fry for 2 minutes. Then add the shiitake mushrooms and fry for 2–3 minutes. Add the beef ribs, increase the heat to high and sear each side for 4–5 minutes, stirring every minute or so. Pour in the sauce, bring to a vigorous boil and continue boiling for 4–5 minutes, stirring every minute or so. Pour in the chicken stock and return to a boil. Reduce the heat to medium-low and simmer, uncovered, for 1½ hours. Then add the carrots, radish, jujube and chestnuts and simmer for another 45 minutes–1 hour until the sauce is reduced and syrupy. The longer you simmer the meat, the more tender it will become, but you may need to add a little hot water every so often if cooking for a much longer period of time. Scatter with the toasted pine nuts, if using, and serve.

4 skinless, boneless chicken
   thighs, sliced into 1cm
   (½ inch) thick strips
½ sweet potato, peeled
   and cut into chips
½ thumb-sized piece
   of ginger, peeled and
   cut into matchsticks
4 garlic cloves, finely chopped
2 spring onions,
   roughly chopped
½ onion, finely sliced
3–4 sweetheart cabbage leaves,
   finely shredded
vegetable oil

MARINADE
2 tablespoons *gochugaru*
   (Korean chilli powder)
¼ teaspoon salt
½ teaspoon sesame oil

SAUCE
50ml (2fl oz) chicken stock
2 tablespoons mirin
1½ tablespoons light soy sauce
1½ tablespoons *gochujang*
   (Korean chilli paste)
1 tablespoon soft brown sugar

SPICY CHICKEN STIR-FRY

This dish reminds me of my old job. I used to work for
a Korean electronics company and the best thing about
the job was the daily free Korean lunch. I would get to work
in the morning and head to the cafe to check what was on
the menu before getting on with the day. There were so many
variations on stir-fried, deep-fried and grilled spicy chicken
dishes, and this dish (*dak galbi*) was cooked in different ways
too. I like the way the freshness and bite of the sweetheart
cabbage balances out the fattiness of the chicken thighs
and sweet chilli flavour of the sauce.

1. Mix the marinade ingredients together then massage the
marinade into the chicken strips.

2. Mix the sauce ingredients together in a jug.

3. **Build Your Wok Clock:** Start at 12 o'clock with the marinated
chicken, followed by the sweet potato, the ginger and garlic,
spring onions, onion, the sauce and lastly the cabbage.

4. Heat 1–2 tablespoons of vegetable oil in a wok to a high
heat. Add the chicken and sear it for 1 minute, pressing down
on the chicken with a spatula so that each piece gets a good
bit of colour, then turn the chicken over and sear the other side
for a minute. Add the sweet potato and stir-fry with the chicken
for 3–4 minutes. Add the ginger and garlic and stir-fry for 30
seconds. Then add the spring onions and onion in turn, stir-frying
for 30 seconds after each addition. Stop stirring for at least
30 seconds to allow the wok to come up to a high heat. Pour
in the sauce and bring to a vigorous boil. Fold the ingredients
through the sauce and stir-fry for a minute or so. Pile the
cabbage on top of the stir-fry and serve.

K
O
R
E
A
N

COFFEE PORK WRAPS

6 tablespoons sea salt
½ head of Chinese leaf
2 litres (3½ pints) cold water
1kg (2lb 4oz) pork belly, with skin, cut into 2cm (¾ inch) thick strips
Radish Salad (see page 164), to serve

BARBECUE SAUCE (SSAMJANG)

4 tablespoons pressed apple juice
2 tablespoons gochujang (Korean chilli paste)
1½ tablespoons honey
1 tablespoon light soy sauce
½ tablespoon Korean soybean paste (swapsies: red miso paste)
1 teaspoon sesame oil
1 tablespoon toasted sesame seeds

POACHING LIQUID

2 onions, cut into wedges
3 spring onions, roughly chopped
1 thumb-sized piece of ginger, peeled and roughly chopped
2 tablespoons Korean soybean paste (swapsies: red miso paste)
1½ tablespoons finely ground filter coffee or instant coffee
1 teaspoon salt
½ tablespoon soft brown sugar
2 litres (3½ pints) chicken stock

In many Asian cuisines, there are certain foods that have specific meanings and are eaten symbolically with the intention of cultivating good fortune. Lettuce or cabbage is often regarded as a lucky food in Korean cuisine, as is also the case in Chinese cuisine and culture. So consider the special significance of this dish when you include it in your feasting menu, offering the wraps (*bossam*) as a gift of good fortune to each of your guests.

1. Rub the sea salt in between each leaf of the half head of Chinese leaf, then soak in the measured cold water for 1 hour to brine. Rinse the leaves under cold running water. Cut off the end of the cabbage stalk and separate the leaves, then pat them dry with kitchen paper, cover them with clingfilm and refrigerate until ready to serve.

2. Blanch the pork belly strips in a large saucepan of boiling water for 5 minutes, then drain and rinse under cold running water to remove any scum or film from the meat.

3. Blitz the *ssamjang* ingredients together in a food processor until smooth.

4. Place the poaching liquid ingredients in a large saucepan and bring to a boil on a high heat. Add the pork belly strips and bring to a vigorous boil, then reduce the heat to medium-low and poach for 1½ hours until the meat is cooked and the edges have taken on some colour from the coffee. Remove from the poaching liquid and slice into 1–2cm (½–¾ inch) thick bite-sized pieces. Serve with the brined leaves for wrapping, with the *ssamjang* on the side along with the Radish Salad.

K
O
R
E
A
N

CRUNCHY VEGGIE STIR-FRY

In my previous School of Wok book, *Delicious Asian Food in Minutes*, you'll find a recipe for different variations on Korean *namul* (seasoned vegetable dishes), which are great palate-cleansers in between bites of the otherwise quite punchy sweet, salty, savoury and spicy dishes that you often find in Korean home cooking. Here's a mixed vegetable dish that provides a quick and simple way to take a break from the stronger flavours your feast, and works perfectly with a spoonful of steamed rice.

1 carrot, cut into matchsticks
2 garlic cloves, finely sliced
handful of Chinese flowering chives (swapsies: green beans), cut into 4-5cm (1½-2 inch) lengths
150g (5½oz) beansprouts, rinsed
200g (7oz) spinach leaves
1 spring onion, cut into matchsticks
2 tablespoons toasted sesame seeds
vegetable oil

SAUCE

2 tablespoons sake (swapsies: rice wine)
1 tablespoon light soy sauce
1 teaspoon sesame oil
¼ teaspoon salt
¼ teaspoon white pepper

1. Mix the sauce ingredients together in a small bowl.

2. **Build Your Wok Clock:** Start at 12 o'clock with the carrot, followed by the garlic, Chinese chives, beansprouts, spinach, the sauce and lastly the spring onion and toasted sesame seeds.

3. Heat ½ tablespoon of vegetable oil in a wok on a high heat until smoking hot. Add the carrot and stir-fry for 30-60 seconds. Add the garlic and then continue working around the wok clock up until the sauce, adding each ingredient in turn and stir-frying for 20-30 seconds after each addition. Then pour in the sauce and bring to a vigorous boil for 30 seconds or so. Scatter with the spring onion and toasted sesame seeds and serve.

KIMCHI PANCAKE

200g (7oz) kimchi,
    roughly chopped
2 spring onions, thinly sliced
¼ onion, thinly sliced
vegetable oil

BATTER

3 tablespoons kimchi liquid
    from the jar
130g (4½oz) plain flour
60g (2¼oz) cornflour
1 teaspoon *gochugaru*
    (Korean chilli powder)
1 egg, lightly beaten
230–250ml (8–9fl oz) cold water

DIPPING SAUCE

1 tablespoon soy sauce
1 tablespoon rice vinegar
1 teaspoon sugar
½ teaspoon sesame seeds
    (optional)
¼ teaspoon *gochugaru*
    (Korean chilli powder)
    (optional)

Kimchi is deeply ingrained in Korean cooking and usually appears in a few different guises. I love the deep red colour that this pancake takes on from the kimchi and its liquid. The combination of textures from the crispy outside and soft, gooey inside adds dimension and interest to any meal. You can make a few smaller, individual pancakes or two or three larger ones as you wish, depending on how much batter you add to the pan at a time.

1. For the batter, put the kimchi liquid into a mixing bowl, followed by the rest of the batter ingredients but only half the measured water at first. Whisk together well. Then gradually add the rest of the water and continue whisking until the mixture reaches the consistency of double cream. Stir in the kimchi, spring onions and onion.

2. Mix the dipping sauce ingredients together in a small bowl.

3. Heat 1–2 tablespoons of vegetable oil in a nonstick frying pan on a medium heat. Add 1–2 ladles of the batter mixture and spread into a thin round pancake. Fry for about 4–5 minutes until the edges turn light golden brown. Carefully flip the pancake over with a spatula, add more oil around the sides of the pan and cook for another 4–5 minutes until golden brown and crispy. Transfer to a serving plate, and keep warm in the oven at 90°C/225°F/Gas Mark ¼. Repeat the process with the remaining batter. Serve immediately with the dipping sauce on the side.

CANDIED MUSHROOMS

20 dried shiitake mushrooms, soaked in hot water for at least 2 hours, preferably overnight, then drained
2 handfuls of dried porcini mushrooms (or any dried mushrooms of your choice), soaked in hot water for at least 2 hours, preferably overnight, then drained
10 tablespoons cornflour, seasoned with ½ teaspoon salt and ¼ teaspoon black pepper
vegetable oil

SAUCE
3 tablespoons mirin
2 tablespoons honey
1½ tablespoons light soy sauce
1 tablespoon rice vinegar
½ tablespoon *gochujang* (Korean chilli paste)

TO GARNISH
1 teaspoon toasted sesame seeds
2 spring onions, finely sliced into rings

Candied snacks are extremely popular in Korea, and these mushrooms are a sweet-savoury version of the traditional *gangjeong*, which are made using deep-fried glutinous rice and often served at celebratory meals. These candied fried mushrooms are a great accompaniment to more savoury and salty dishes.

1. Squeeze any excess water out of all the soaked mushrooms and then press them firmly with kitchen paper to dry them.

2. Fill a tray with the seasoned cornflour. Add all the mushrooms and toss them in the cornflour, making sure that each is well coated, dry to the touch and dusty white in colour. If necessary, add a few more tablespoons of cornflour to fully coat the mushrooms.

3. Mix the sauce ingredients together in a bowl.

4. Fill a wok one-third full with oil and bring to a medium-high heat. Test the temperature by placing the tip of a wooden chopstick in the oil. If it starts to fizz after a second, the oil has reached the desired temperature.

5. Carefully lay the mushrooms in the hot oil and fry them for about 3–4 minutes until golden brown – it's worth frying them in 2–3 batches to ensure they are all as crispy as possible. Remove with a slotted spoon and place them on a plate lined with kitchen paper to drain the excess oil.

6. Carefully pour the hot oil from the wok into a heatproof bowl or saucepan, leave to cool, then discard. Meanwhile, reheat the wok on a high heat until smoking hot. Pour in the sauce, bring to a vigorous boil and continue boiling for 3–4 minutes until reduced and syrupy. Add the fried mushrooms and fold them through until the sauce has completely coated them. Scatter with the toasted sesame seeds and spring onions and serve.

RADISH SALAD

1 Korean radish (swapsies: daikon), peeled and cut into matchsticks

DRESSING
1½ tablespoons *gochugaru* (Korean chilli powder)
½ tablespoon soft brown sugar
2 garlic cloves, finely chopped
2 spring onions, finely sliced into rings
1 tablespoon vegetarian fish sauce (swapsies: fish sauce or light soy sauce)
2 teaspoons rice vinegar
1 teaspoon salt

There are many types of radish salad in Korean cuisine, and traditionally one made with fermented oysters and prawns would be served alongside the Coffee Pork Wraps (see page 158). This salad, however, is a quick and simple version that requires no fermentation, can easily be made vegan and provides a great crunch and spice balance to the meal. In fact, it makes the perfect addition to any Korean feast.

1. Mix the dressing ingredients together in a bowl, then add the radish and massage the marinade into the radish.

2. Leave to marinate for at least 15 minutes before serving.

FISH OMELETTE PARCELS

3 eggs
1 spring onion, finely chopped
½ red chilli, finely chopped
½ teaspoon salt
¼ teaspoon white pepper
6–10 tablespoons plain flour
400g (14oz) firm white fish fillets
   (such as cod, hake, haddock
   or pollock), skin removed and
   cut into 3cm (1¼ inch) slices
vegetable oil

DIPPING SAUCE
½ tablespoon *gochugaru*
   (Korean chilli powder)
1 garlic clove, finely chopped
1 spring onion, finely sliced
   into rings
1 tablespoon vegetable oil
2 tablespoons light soy sauce
1 tablespoon mirin
1 teaspoon sesame oil
½ tablespoon toasted
   sesame seeds

Eggs are one of those few ingredients that are so versatile that they have a place in almost every cuisine around the globe. They provide simple solutions to quick midweek meals, but also work as an effortless way to fill in the gaps of a feast. By getting inventive when it comes to cooking eggs, you could easily add another hundred dishes to your feasting repertoire! The classic version of this dish (*daegujeon*) uses thinner pieces of fish, but I love the shapes you get with larger chunks and the extra-crispy edges from the dollops of egg mixture added when frying them.

1. Beat the eggs together in a mixing bowl, then season with the spring onion, chilli, salt and pepper and mix well.

2. For the dipping sauce, mix the chilli powder, garlic and spring onion together in a heatproof bowl or ramekin. Heat the vegetable oil in a small saucepan on a medium heat until smoking hot. Turn off the heat and wait for 30 seconds before pouring over the chilli powder, garlic and spring onion. Add the rest of the dipping sauce ingredients and mix together.

3. Fill a tray with the flour. Add the fish pieces and toss in the flour until well coated. Then dip each floured fish piece in turn into the beaten egg mixture and lay on a plate ready to fry.

4. Heat 3 tablespoons of vegetable oil in a large frying pan to a medium heat. Place the coated fish pieces, one at a time, in the hot oil, allowing at least 5mm (¼ inch) in between each piece, and fry for 1 minute. Then pour an additional 1–2 tablespoons of the egg mixture over each fish piece and fry for another 2–3 minutes until golden brown on the underside. Turn over and fry the other side for 1–2 minutes. Then flip the pieces over and spoon a little of the hot oil over the top of each piece 3–4 times, continuing to cook for a further minute, until golden brown and cooked through. Carefully transfer to a serving plate and serve immediately with the dipping sauce on the side.

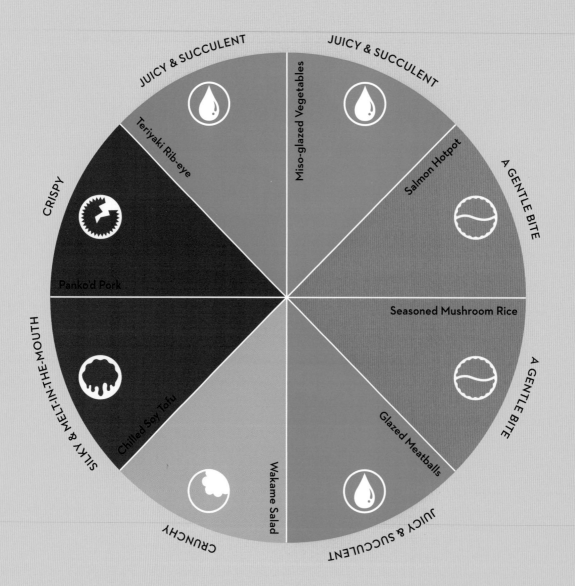

JUICY & SUCCULENT

JUICY & SUCCULENT

Miso-glazed Vegetables

Salmon Hotpot

A GENTLE BITE

Teriyaki Rib-eye

CRISPY

Panko'd Pork

Seasoned Mushroom Rice

A GENTLE BITE

SILKY & MELT-IN-THE-MOUTH

Chilled Soy Tofu

Glazed Meatballs

Wakame Salad

JUICY & SUCCULENT

CRUNCHY

JAPANESE

I have been lucky in the past to have enjoyed some of the best food sitting at sushi counters in beautifully serene Japanese restaurants, witnessing the theatre of the chefs' meticulously learned knife skills and super-precise hand movements. These days, however, my (and my children's) stomach-to-brain patience is just not well trained enough to wait the time needed to perfect some of the finest dishes of Japanese cuisine. So for now at least, it's probably best that as a family we eat Japanese food at home, and therefore I must cook it myself.

When it comes to Japanese cuisine, most people instinctively picture extravagant platters of delicately prepared sushi or sashimi. But there is a whole world of home-cooked recipes simple enough to make without years of training. I liken these home-style Japanese dishes to a minimalistic Japanese garden – well pruned yet still perfectly at one with nature – as in the Salmon Hotpot (see page 182), where the vegetables and fish are cut to fit the pot perfectly and the main stock flavour comes from a simple dashi. It highlights a few great-quality ingredients with some well-balanced, simple seasoning. In Japanese food, the freshness of the ingredients is paramount, even for something as simple as a sweetcorn cob. Go to the market, buy a proper cob with its leaves and take the time to peel away the layers to get to the sweetness; whenever you can make the extra effort, it's always worthwhile.

Your precision mustn't stop there, as even your pans can elevate the natural earthiness of a dish. If you ever need a new pan, or someone has asked what you want for your birthday, consider some Japanese earthenware. These clay pots are designed specifically to sit directly on the hob, adding beautifully earthy notes to anything cooked within. Getting into the mindset of fewer-but-better-quality things whenever possible pays off.

Serving a Japanese meal at home can also be a lot of fun. If you take the task on, I urge you to channel your inner sense of respect and organization, lining everything up and dressing the table with small pots of soy sauce or simple side salads for added balance in flavour, colour and texture. Make sure those balancing salads are portioned out accordingly so that each guest is within easy reach; it might seem pedantic, but there's a certain level of satisfaction you will get from approaching your feast in this new meticulous way.

When making your Japanese feast, the daikon in the Miso-glazed Vegetables requires time to soften, so you may as well prepare the whole dish and get the miso glaze onto the precooked aubergine and tofu ready to grill at serving time. Approach the Salmon Hotpot in two stages: first, boil the dashi and broth and prep your Wok Clock, then return to the recipe when ready to eat, reheating the broth and finishing the dish off. Cook the Seasoned Mushroom Rice on the hob, or in a rice cooker if you have one, then form the Glazed Meatballs. Once the meatballs are made, they are easy to fry (or grill) for 10–15 minutes before serving up the rest of the meal. Get all the ingredients for the Wakame Salad prepared and sitting in separate airtight containers with the dressing covered on the side, then keep in the fridge so that you can serve it crisp and clean without any hassle. Similarly, the Chilled Soy Tofu is easily prepared in advance – again, just keep all the prepared ingredients separate and covered in the fridge until ready to compile and serve. Next, prepare the Panko'd Pork to get the messy breadcrumbing process and deep-frying out of the way before addressing the rest of the meal. Leave the Teriyaki Rib-eye, if cooking, until last – even with a little resting time, steak is always best kept to the end of any meal preparation to make sure it's served as fresh as possible.

WAKAME SALAD

50g (1¾oz) dried wakame
seaweed, soaked in hot
water for 15 minutes
1 carrot, cut into matchsticks
¼ cucumber, cut
into matchsticks
handful of radishes, finely sliced
1 tablespoon toasted
sesame seeds

DRESSING
⅓ thumb-sized piece of ginger,
peeled and grated or
finely chopped
1 garlic clove, grated or
finely chopped
½ teaspoon sugar
2 tablespoons Japanese
soy sauce
1½ tablespoons mirin
1 tablespoon rice vinegar
½ tablespoon sesame oil

Dried seaweed of all types is a must when venturing into Japanese cooking at home. While it's renowned for its high nutritional value and has a natural unique salty flavour, it is the texture of seaweed that really excites me. Although many would describe it as slimy, I think there's a lot more crunch and bite to seaweed when you consider the entire eating experience. Similar to jellyfish, another common and much-loved food in Asia prized primarily for its texture, there's an initial slippery quality when it first touches your palate, but when bitten into, the crunchiness creates an addictive mouthfeel that gets your taste buds coming back for more pretty quickly.

1. Drain the soaked wakame seaweed and tear it into bite-sized pieces.

2. Once prepared, place the vegetables in separate bowls of ice-cold water until ready to serve to prevent discolouration and wilting, then drain well.

3. Mix the dressing ingredients together in a small bowl.

4. Arrange the salad as you wish and pour over the dressing or toss everything together with the dressing, then serve.

JAPANESE

MISO-GLAZED VEGETABLES

1 sheet of kombu, soaked in
 1 litre (1¾ pints) cold water,
 seasoned with 1 teaspoon
 sea salt, for at least 2 hours,
 preferably overnight,
 in the fridge
1 daikon, peeled and sliced
 into 4–5cm (1½–2 inch)
 thick rounds
2 aubergines
300g (10½oz) fresh firm tofu
vegetable oil

MISO *DENGAKU* GLAZE
175g (6oz) red or white
 miso paste
5 tablespoons sake
2 tablespoons mirin
2 tablespoons sugar
2 egg yolks

Nasu dengaku (miso aubergine) is currently the most popular version of this dish, named *dengaku* after a folk dance traditionally performed during seasonal rice-planting celebrations as a form of prayer asking the gods of rice to provide highly fertile crops. Nowadays the dance can be seen at various cultural celebrations and festivals. The miso glaze works a treat with tofu, aubergine or daikon. If you have time, cook all three for a fantastic balance of texture and flavour.

1. Place the daikon pieces in the kombu water (dashi) in a pan and bring to a boil on a high heat, then reduce the heat to medium and simmer for 20 minutes, then remove to cool.

2. Meanwhile, slice the aubergines into 2cm (¾ inch) thick rounds, then score the top of each round with a criss-cross pattern. Rub with 2 tablespoons of vegetable oil. Cut the fresh tofu into 3cm (1¼ inch) long rectangles, 1cm (½ inch) and place on a few sheets of kitchen paper to absorb any excess liquid.

3. For the miso *dengaku* glaze, mix the miso paste, sake, mirin and sugar together in a small saucepan on a medium heat. Bring to a boil for 2–3 minutes, then remove from the heat for 1–2 minutes. Add the egg yolks and mix into the glaze.

4. Heat a frying pan to a medium heat, add the aubergine rounds and fry for 4–5 minutes on each side until lightly browned and softened, about 80% cooked – you should be able to push the tip of a sharp knife or fork gently into the flesh with very little resistance. Spread ½ tablespoon of the glaze over the scored side of each round and place in a lightly oiled roasting tray.

5. Heat 1 tablespoon of vegetable oil in the frying pan to a medium heat and fry the tofu pieces for 3–4 minutes on each side until golden brown. Spread ½ tablespoon of the glaze on one side of each tofu piece and place in a separate lightly oiled roasting tray.

6. Place the aubergine and tofu trays under a grill on a high heat for 5 minutes until the glaze is gently charred and caramelized. Before serving, remove the daikon from the dashi, dollop ½ tablespoon of the glaze over each piece and serve all together.

GLAZED MEATBALLS

vegetable oil

MEATBALLS
4 boneless chicken thighs,
    with skin, roughly chopped
    into chunks (swapsies: minced
    pork or chicken)
3 spring onions, roughly
    chopped
½ thumb-sized piece of ginger,
    peeled and roughly chopped
2 tablespoons sesame seeds
½ teaspoon salt
¼ teaspoon white pepper
1 egg yolk, lightly beaten
1 tablespoon light soy sauce

***TARE* SAUCE**
6 spring onions, halved
1–2 teaspoons soft brown sugar
100ml (3½fl oz) water
4–5 tablespoons Japanese light
    soy sauce
3 tablespoons sake
3 tablespoons mirin

Feeding kids is a full-time job and I often get a bit of dad guilt when there are days in a row where the responsibility falls solely on my wife. But when I get the chance to do some experimental catering for my kids, I try to work out the patterns in their episodes of eating with gusto (which, however infrequent they may be, do seem to occur from time to time), and I recently discovered that my one-year-old loves meatballs of any kind. So *tsukune*, essentially a Japanese meatball, is now a go-to, as the pantry ingredients are always within easy reach and the sweet–savoury glaze makes your mouth water, no matter what your age!

1. Soak 10–15 bamboo skewers in water for 10 minutes.

2. Place the chicken pieces in a food processor along with the rest of the meatball ingredients and pulse for 1–2 minutes into a smooth paste (you may need to stop the machine a few times to push the mixture back down before blitzing again).

3. Have a bowl of cold water nearby to dampen your hands to avoid the mixture sticking to them, then shape the meatball mixture into golf ball-sized meatballs. Slide the meatballs onto the presoaked skewers and press them gently into sausage shapes, then set them aside on a tray ready to cook.

4. Mix the *tare* sauce ingredients together in a saucepan and bring to boil on a medium heat for 2 minutes, then reduce the heat to low and simmer for 5–10 minutes.

5. Heat 1–2 tablespoons of vegetable oil in a large frying pan to a medium-high heat, place the meatball skewers in the hot oil and fry for a minute or so to sear on one side. Reduce the heat to medium and fry on the same side for another 4–5 minutes while brushing the meatballs with a generous amount of the *tare*. Increase the heat to medium-high, turn the skewers over and sear the other side for about a minute. Then again reduce the heat to medium and fry for another 3–4 minutes while brushing the meatballs with more of the *tare*. About 1–2 minutes before serving, pour the rest of the tare over the meatballs to give them a good glaze. Serve warm.

PANKO'D PORK

4 pork shoulder steaks,
   about 150g (5½oz) each,
   and 2cm (¾ inch) thick
100g (3½oz) plain flour,
   seasoned with a pinch
   of salt and pepper
2 eggs
150g (5½oz) panko
   breadcrumbs
vegetable oil
2–3 sweetheart cabbage leaves,
   finely shredded, to serve

RED ONION PICKLE

1 red onion, finely sliced
   into rings
5 tablespoons rice vinegar
½ teaspoon salt
1 tablespoon sugar

MARINADE

2 garlic cloves, finely chopped
½ thumb-sized piece of ginger,
   peeled and finely chopped
2 tablespoons sake
2 tablespoons Japanese
   soy sauce

TONKATSU SAUCE

2 tablespoons mushroom
   stir-fry sauce or oyster sauce
3 tablespoons
   Worcestershire sauce
2 tablespoons tomato ketchup
3 teaspoons sugar

The perfect crispy component to any feast, this dish is easily shared between many when sliced into strips and served along with a few other dishes. However, if you just have a hankering for breaded deep-fried pork (*tonkatsu*) halfway through the week, I don't blame you! In fact, I'd suggest you get a couple of thick slices of inexpensive white bread, butter and toast them in a dry frying pan, then plonk everything from the recipe – pickles, cabbage and all – between them slathered with the *tonkatsu* sauce for a simple and deeply satisfying *katsu* sando.

1. Mix the pickle ingredients together until the sugar dissolves.

2. Mix the marinade ingredients together, then massage the marinade into the pork steaks.

3. Mix the *tonkatsu* sauce ingredients together in a saucepan and bring to a boil for 30–60 seconds until the sugar has melted and the sauce has lightly caramelized.

4. Set up 3 shallow bowls for dredging: place the seasoned flour in one, beat the eggs together well in the second and place the panko breadcrumbs in the third. Dip the marinated pork steaks into the seasoned flour until well coated and shake off any excess, then dip them into the beaten egg and let any excess drip off before dipping them into the panko, covering the meat completely. Set aside on a plate. Repeat the dredging process if you want a thicker coating of breadcrumbs.

5. Half-fill a large saucepan, wok or deep-fryer with vegetable oil and bring to a medium-high heat. Test the temperature of the oil by placing the tip of a wooden chopstick or skewer in the oil. If it starts to fizz after a second or so, the oil has reached the desired temperature of around 180°C/350°F. Carefully lay the pork steaks in the hot oil and deep-fry for 7–8 minutes until golden brown and crispy. Alternatively, heat 10 tablespoons of vegetable oil in a large frying pan to a medium-high heat and fry the steaks, turning once, for 10–12 minutes until golden brown and cripsy. Work in batches and keep them warm in the oven at 90°C/225°F/Gas Mark ¼, if necessary. Cut the pork into slices and serve with the shredded cabbage, red onion pickle and *tonkatsu* sauce on the side.

SEASONED MUSHROOM RICE

2 cups of Japanese rice
(I use a 240ml/8½fl oz cup,
holding 195g/7oz rice)
2 cups (see above) of cold water
150g (5½oz) shiitake
mushrooms, sliced
150g (5½oz) shimeji
mushrooms, separated
150g (5½oz) enoki mushrooms,
roughly chopped
150g (5½oz) oyster mushrooms,
roughly torn into chunks
vegetable oil
1 spring onion, finely sliced
into rings, to garnish

SEASONING
2 tablespoons Japanese
soy sauce
1 tablespoon mirin
1 tablespoon sake
½ teaspoon salt
½ teaspoon soft brown sugar

A good Japanese friend of mine from university days lived in a bedsit studio above a cute little cottage. Given his limited kitchen space, I was always impressed by the food he would cook using just a rice cooker and a one-ring plug-in ceramic hob. Each meal, however simple, would be served up bento style on a special sectioned plate, with a designated place for the rice, another for the perfectly seasoned protein and a washed and dried crispy salad on the side. I so admired the respect he showed when making and presenting food, and the value placed on this care and attention in Japanese culture. I like to sear the mushrooms for a more concentrated mushroom flavour from their caramelized edges, but if you want a one-pot wonder rice dish with zero faff, then simply plonk it all in a rice cooker and let it do its thing!

1. Wash the rice at least 3 times. Place the rice in a bowl and run it under cold water, gently moving the rice grains between the tips of your fingers. The excess starch from the rice grains will initially make the water quite cloudy, so pour the rice through a sieve in between each wash. By the end of the washing process, the water should run clear. Sieve one last time and place the rice in a saucepan with the measured water. Add the seasoning ingredients and stir well. Cover with a tight-fitting lid and set aside for 30 minutes to allow the rice to absorb some of the water.

2. Heat 1 tablespoon of vegetable oil in a frying pan to a high heat. Add all the mushrooms, press down on them with a spatula and sear them for 1–2 minutes until golden brown. Turn them over and sear the other side. Transfer the mushrooms to the rice pan and replace the lid.

3. Place the pan on a medium-high heat and bring to a vigorous boil. Then reduce the heat to low and simmer with the lid on for 12–15 minutes until the liquid has fully evaporated to the point where you start to see air pockets form in between some of the rice grains. Replace the lid, turn the heat off and leave the rice to sit for another 15 minutes. Scatter with the spring onions to garnish and serve.

½ onion, cut into wedges
1 sweetcorn cob, quartered
1 potato, peeled and cut
    into large chunks
½ daikon, peeled and
    cut into large chunks
¼ sweetheart cabbage,
    cut into wedges
5–6 shiitake mushrooms
200g (7oz) medium silken tofu,
    cut into bite-sized cubes
300g (10½oz) skinless salmon
    fillet, cut into 1cm (½ inch)
    thick slices
100g (3½oz) watercress
2 spring onions,
    sliced diagonally

DASHI
1 sheet of kombu seaweed
1 litre (1¾ pints) cold water,
    seasoned with ½ teaspoon
    sea salt

MISO BUTTER
4 tablespoons salted butter,
    at room temperature
3 tablespoons miso
3 tablespoons sake
1 tablespoon mirin
½ tablespoon Japanese
    soy sauce

SALMON HOTPOT

As Jenny Linford writes about in her book *The Missing Ingredient*, the ingredient that makes this dish so wonderful is the time it takes to make it. Taking your time by poaching ingredients in a broth like this allows the flavours to develop, each ingredient adding its own natural sweetness to it. As well as sweetening the broth, here the sweetcorn also absorbs the savoury flavour from the subtle dashi through the simmering process. The hotpot (*donabe*) might be regarded as a wintery recipe, but the ultimate comforting nourishment it provides makes it appropriate for any time of the year.

1. For the dashi, place the kombu in a bowl covered with the seasoned water and leave to soak for at least 2 hours, preferably overnight in the fridge.

2. Beat the miso butter ingredients together in a bowl into a smooth paste, then cover and refrigerate for 1 hour until firm.

3. **Build Your Wok Clock:** Start at 12 o'clock with the dashi, the onion, sweetcorn, potato and daikon, followed by the cabbage and shiitake mushrooms, tofu and salmon, watercress and spring onions and lastly the miso butter.

4. Transfer the dashi (including the kombu) to a large clay pot or cast-iron pan and bring to a boil on a medium-high heat, then reduce the heat to medium, add the onion, sweetcorn, potato and daikon and simmer for 25–30 minutes.

5. Remove the kombu from the dashi, add the cabbage and shiitake mushrooms and simmer for 5 minutes. Next add the tofu and salmon and simmer for 3–4 minutes. Just before serving, add the watercress and spring onions, then increase the heat to high, cut the miso butter into chunks and add them to the pan for a final 1–2 minutes, allowing the liquid to boil before immediately removing the pot from the heat to serve.

TERIYAKI RIB-EYE

300g (10½oz) rib-eye steak
½ thumb-sized piece
   of ginger, peeled and
   cut into matchsticks
2 spring onions, roughly
   chopped into 5cm
   (2 inch) lengths
vegetable oil

MARINADE
4 tablespoons Japanese
   soy sauce
4 tablespoons mirin
4 tablespoons sake
1 tablespoon dark soy sauce
1 tablespoon sugar

Serving up a good steak can be a joyful and luxurious way to mark a special occasion. The beauty of cooking steak is that it must be done quickly, but in your preparations for the feast, make sure you allow for the fact that you will need to leave cooking it to the last minute to avoid ruining your treat. You can create a wonderful Japanese sharing meal by serving a few slices of this steak with the Seasoned Mushroom Rice (see page 180) and the Wakame Salad (see page 174) on the side. However, you may want to keep it just for yourself to savour and think about treating your friends to a dish that you don't have to fight them over!

1. Mix the marinade ingredients together in a mixing bowl, then add the steak and massage the marinade into meat.

2. Heat a griddle pan or frying pan to a high heat and then brush the pan with vegetable oil. Add the steak to the hot pan and cook for 3–4 minutes on each side until well charred and caramelized on both sides.

3. A minute before your steak is cooked to your liking, add the ginger and spring onions to the pan and briefly sear, then pour in the remaining marinade and allow to boil vigorously for 30–60 seconds, depending on how well done you want your steak.

4. Transfer the steak to a chopping board and allow to rest for 2–3 minutes, then slice diagonally into thin strips. Reduce the marinade for another minute or so, then pour over the steak strips to serve.

J
A
P
A
N
E
S
E

CHILLED SOY TOFU

2 × 300g (10½oz) blocks
 of chilled soft silken tofu
½ cucumber, finely sliced
 or peeled into ribbons
 with a vegetable peeler
1 thumb-sized piece of ginger,
 peeled and finely grated
2 tablespoons toasted sesame
 seeds or small handful of
 bonito flakes (optional)
100ml (3½fl oz) Japanese
 soy sauce
100ml (3½fl oz) dashi,
 ready-made or homemade
 (see page 182) (optional)
½ small daikon, grated, to serve
4 spring onions, finely sliced
 into rings, to serve

This one is for my awesome friend and genius photographer of all my delicious recipes Kris Kirkham, as it's one of his favourite dishes to prepare and eat. Much like his photography, it's simple, bright, flavourful and striking to look at. The melt-in-the-mouth texture of the silken tofu speaks for itself and provides a balance across any large feast or simple midweek meal.

1. Cut each block of tofu in half into 2 large cubes and place each cube in a serving bowl.

2. Arrange the cucumber slices or ribbons carefully over the tofu, then top with the grated ginger and scatter with the toasted sesame seeds or bonito flakes, if using. Just before serving, pour the Japanese soy sauce and dashi, if using, over the top of the tofu, and serve with grated daikon and spring onions on the side.

DESSERTS

A feast is not really a feast without something sweet to finish it off. Asian desserts aren't talked about enough in the West, which I find surprising, as there are so many dessert houses, lounges and designated cafes across Asia. There are even huge dessert buffets in some of the big hotels that are so famous for their sweets that people plan their whole eating day around reserving enough stomach capacity for a feastful of cakes, sweet tofu, matcha pancakes and more.

In Malaysia, people queue up at their favourite local ice *kacang* stalls for a pile of colourful and cooling shaved ice with all their favourite toppings (see page 202), while Indonesia has several layered cakes and jellies that are to die for. Singapore is bursting with bakeries and sweet-treat cafes, so much so that it's hard to walk down a street and not feel hungry just from the smell of freshly baked cakes. In Vietnam and the Philippines, the condensed milk and syrupy coffees could be considered desserts in themselves, let alone all the flans, brûlées and various versions of crème caramel (see page 192) that are served alongside them. The Thais take to their sweets on the streets, where there are pit stops dotted around street-food stands and market stalls. And in Japan, China and Korea, there's a shared love for perfect versions of fluffy baked cheesecakes (see page 200), Swiss rolls and sponge cakes of all different sizes, flavours and colours. All across Asian cultures, eating sweets is a social event in itself, not just something confined to the end of a meal.

There are recipes in this chapter for every occasion. All are fun, moreish and deserve their place on the world stage of sweets, so I urge you to give them a try. It's high time more Asian desserts become celebrated for their place in each cuisine, so I'm hoping some of these recipes might just have that effect.

COFFEE & COCONUT FLAN

CARAMEL
300g (10½oz) caster sugar
300ml (10fl oz) water

CUSTARD
6 large eggs, at room
  temperature
400ml (14oz) coconut milk
300ml (10fl oz) condensed milk
1 shot of strong espresso
  (swapsies: 2 tablespoons
  good-quality instant coffee
  dissolved in 1 tablespoon
  hot water)

whipped cream, fresh fruit or
  sugared peanuts, to decorate

Of all the sweet dishes in the world, you wouldn't expect the simple flan to be so well travelled. Yet when you look at the simplicity of its ingredients – essentially a sweetened and flavoured egg custard – you can see why so many cultures have adopted the flan into their own cuisines. This coffee-flavoured version is found in most coffee shops in Vietnam, but it's also one of the most popular desserts in the Philippines.

1. Stand 10 ramekins in an ovenproof dish or deep-sided baking tray. Preheat the oven to 160°C/350°F/Gas Mark 4.

2. For the caramel, place the sugar and water in a saucepan on a low heat and stir for 3–4 minutes until the sugar fully dissolves. Increase the heat to high and allow the sugar syrup to boil vigorously, without stirring, for about 5–6 minutes until it reaches a rich golden brown colour, taking care to ensure it doesn't burn. Once ready, carefully and without hesitation, divide the caramel between the ramekins to form a layer of caramel on the base of each one.

3. For the custard, crack the eggs into a large mixing bowl, add the coconut milk and condensed milk and beat well to form a thick smooth mixture. Add the coffee and stir in, then strain the custard through a fine mesh sieve into a jug. Divide evenly between the ramekins.

4. Pour boiling water into the ovenproof dish until level with the top of the custard in the ramekins, being careful not to get any in the flans. Bake for 45 minutes–1 hour, depending on size, until set. Remove from the oven and allow to cool slightly, then remove the ramekins from the hot water, taking care not to burn yourself. Allow to cool completely before serving.

5. To serve, loosen the rim of each flan using a dampened finger and then turn out onto a serving plate. Decorate with whipped cream, fresh fruit or sugared peanuts.

MACANESE EGG TARTS

unsalted butter, melted,
    for greasing
320g (11¼oz) all-butter
    puff pastry sheet
plain flour, for dusting
icing sugar, for dusting

EGG CUSTARD
3 medium eggs
250ml (9fl oz) semi-skimmed
    milk
100g (3½oz) caster sugar
1 cinnamon stick
1 tablespoon evaporated milk
1 teaspoon vanilla extract

This in-betweener of an egg tart sits somewhere among the English, Portuguese and Hong Kong versions. When baked in a muffin tray like this, there's a wonderful depth to the tarts, allowing plenty of space for the custard mixture to wobble its way out when you bite into them, making the experience extra satisfying and indulgent. Best eaten straight out of the oven!

1. For the egg custard, beat the eggs together well in a large jug.

2. Place the milk, caster sugar and cinnamon stick in a saucepan on a medium heat and stir for 3–4 minutes until the sugar fully dissolves. Remove from the heat and allow to cool slightly. Remove the cinnamon stick and gradually pour the warm milk over the beaten eggs while whisking continously. Then add the evaporated milk and vanilla extract and whisk well. Cover the surface of the egg custard with clingfilm to prevent a skin from forming and refrigerate for 1 hour.

3. Meanwhile, brush inside the cups of a 12-cup muffin tray with melted butter. Using a rolling pin or clean wine bottle, roll the puff pastry sheet out on a lightly floured work surface to about 2mm (1/16 inch) thick. Roll the pastry up like a Swiss roll and then cut it into 12 equal wheels about 2–3cm (¾–1¼ inches) thick. Press each wheel down in turn with the palm of your hand to flatten and then press into a greased muffin cup to line it until the sides just overlap the cup edges.

4. Preheat the oven to 220°C/475°F/Gas Mark 9. Pour the egg custard into the muffin cups until they are just over three-quarters full. Carefully transfer the muffin tray to the oven and bake for 15–20 minutes until browned on the top. Gently remove from the oven and allow to cool in the muffin tray, then dust the tarts with icing sugar to serve.

SWEET ROTI

150g (5½oz) unsalted butter,
    for making the ghee
    (clarified butter), see below
caster sugar, to serve

DOUGH
400g (14oz) plain flour
    or strong bread flour,
    plus extra for dusting
1 egg
½ tablespoon honey
    or condensed milk
½ teaspoon salt
ghee (clarified butter)
    from method below
225–250ml (8–9fl oz) warm water

TO MAKE THE GHEE
Place the butter in a heatproof
mixing bowl and set over
a saucepan of hot water. Heat
the pan on a medium heat
until the butter has melted and
separated into a clear layer on
top and a milky residue below.
Refrigerate for about 1 hour
until the clarified butter on top
has solidified, then pierce a hole
through the clarified butter and
discard the milky residue below,
reserving the solidified, clarified
butter (ghee). Store in the
fridge in a sealed container until
ready to use. It will easily soften
in your hands when you come
to use it.

In the hawker stalls of Malaysia, the masters of this dish have
amazingly soft hands, as they are constantly covered in ghee.
The more ghee you have on your hands, the better the roti. I
have fond memories of being on holiday in Malaysia as a child
and my dad would present us with a stack of freshly made *roti
canai* – crispy on the outside and flaky on the inside with sugar
crystals melting over the top – each morning. Heaven!

1. For the dough, place the flour in a mixing bowl and make a
well in the centre. Add the egg, honey or condensed milk, salt,
4 tablespoons of ghee and half the water to the well and start
to mix in the flour. Add a little more water and bring the mixture
together into a dough. Gradually add water while you use your
other hand to knead the dough into a ball until all the flour from
the edges has been incorporated and you have a plasticine-like
dough. Knead the dough on a lightly floured work surface for
3–4 minutes until smooth. Form into a ball, rub 1 tablespoon
of ghee over the dough ball and place back in the mixing bowl.
Cover with a damp tea towel or clingfilm and allow to rest for
5 minutes.

2. Divide the dough into 10 smooth balls. Soften 1 tablespoon of
ghee in your hands and cover the balls with it, then place them
in a roasting tray. Cover with clingfilm and refrigerate overnight.

3. Remove the dough from the fridge and leave for 30 minutes
to return to room temperature. Press down each ball in turn with
your palm and spread out thinly, then carefully flip the pastry
over and continue to press down and thin out until you can see
the work surface through it. Rub ½ a tablespoon of ghee over
the top, then push the pastry inwards from opposite sides to
form a rippled log. Curl the log up like a snail shell, tucking the
end into the centre to create a swirl. Just before cooking, flatten
the swirls and press out with your palms and thumbs again until
roughly 15cm (6 inches) in diameter and 2mm (1/16 inch) thick.

4. Heat a dry frying pan to medium heat, add one roti at a time
and fry for about 3–4 minutes on both sides until crispy and
golden brown, stacking the roti to keep them warm. Top with
a slather of ghee and a generous scattering of sugar to serve.

PEANUT & SESAME MOCHI

PEANUT MIXTURE
4 tablespoons ground salted
    roasted peanuts
2 tablespoons toasted
    sesame seeds
2 tablespoons toasted
    desiccated coconut
    (see below) (optional)
1 tablespoon caster sugar
a pinch of sea salt

DOUGH
150g (5½oz) glutinous rice
    flour (sweet rice flour)
50g (1¾oz) caster sugar
3 tablespoons icing sugar
1 teaspoon cocoa powder,
    matcha tea powder or vanilla
    extract (or ⅓ teaspoon of
    all 3 so you can make a mix
    of mochi as we have here)
240ml (8½fl oz) water

TO TOAST THE COCONUT
Toast the desiccated coconut
in a dry frying pan on a medium
heat for 4-5 minutes, stirring
or tossing, until fragrant and
uniformly golden brown.
Allow to cool.

Mochi brings back memories of long ago when we spent our summer holidays in and out of Hong Kong visiting my grandma. If my Uncle Janga happened to be around we would head down to the local 7-Eleven and load a basket with every flavour of *mochi* ice cream they had in stock, twice over. This dessert that the Japanese made world famous originated from the simple glutinous rice pastries of ancient China, which were filled with red bean paste and deep-fried or boiled. In Hong Kong and South East Asia, the street-food version is made in the same way as here, except steamed rather than microwaved. Sweet and slightly salty with a little crunch on the outside, these sticky little balls of dough are heavenly.

1. Blitz the peanut mixture ingredients in a food processor to form a fine dry powder, but take care not to overwork or the oil from the peanuts will start to be released. Transfer to a mixing bowl.

2. Mix the dough ingredients together in a microwave-safe bowl with a wooden spoon or spatula until the mixture is uniform in texture, with no lumps of flour. Cover with clingfilm and microwave on high power (1000W) for 1½ minutes. Remove from the microwave and stir vigorously for a minute or so. The dough will probably be relatively runny still, but once well stirred it should stiffen up. Replace the clingfilm and microwave for another minute. Remove and stir vigorously again until smooth. If your microwave is lower-powered, repeat the process another 2-3 times in 30-second bursts until you have a sticky, doughy consistency. Allow the dough to sit for 5 minutes before handling it, as it will be extremely hot.

3. Have a bowl of cold water nearby to dampen your hands to prevent the mixture from sticking to them and a tablespoon dipped in it ready to scoop the dough. Scoop out ½ a tablespoon or so of the dough, dampen your hands and roll the dough between your palms into a rough ball, then place in the bowl with the peanut mixture. Continue until you have 6-8 balls of dough in the peanut mixture, then toss them through the mixture to coat and serve. Repeat the process with the rest of the dough, then serve.

CANTONESE BAKED SPONGE

SPONGE MIXTURE
4 egg yolks
2 tablespoons caster sugar
40ml (8 teaspoons) full-fat milk
2 tablespoons vegetable oil
70g (2½oz) plain flour
¼ teaspoon baking powder

MERINGUE
4 egg whites
¼ teaspoon cream of tartar
3 tablespoons caster sugar

Specific foods remind me of certain people, and I find that these foods are a fantastic way to bring a memory of that person's face immediately to mind. It's because when someone digs into that special slice of cake, or crispy bite of pork belly, their smug food face lingers long in my thoughts. This recipe conjures up a vivid picture of my best mate Mark's food face, standing in front of a Cantonese bakery wherever in the world – Hong Kong, London's Chinatown – with an expression of pure happiness, the dim sum he just stuffed down him completely forgotten as he euphorically bites into the sweet, fluffy, cloudy, pillowy dreaminess of a confection.

1. Preheat the oven to 165°C/360°F/Gas Mark 4½. Line a 12-cup muffin tray with squares of baking paper or tulip muffin cases.

2. For the sponge mixture, beat the egg yolks and sugar together in a large mixing bowl with a whisk until slightly fluffy and pale yellow in colour. Add the milk and vegetable oil and continue to whisk gently until smooth. Sift in the flour and baking powder and gently fold into the mixture with a large metal spoon.

3. For the meringue, place the egg whites with the cream of tartar in a large, extremely clean mixing bowl (wipe with a little white vinegar or rice vinegar to be sure) and whisk until soft peaks form. Then add 1 tablespoon of the caster sugar at a time, whisking well after each addition. Continue whisking until stiff, silky smooth and glossy.

4. Add 1 heaped tablespoon of the meringue to the sponge mixture and beat well to loosen the mixture. Then continue adding the rest of the meringue, 1 tablespoon at a time but folding in gently after each addition.

5. Spoon the sponge mixture evenly into each of the muffin cases until they are three-quarters full. Bake for 25 minutes until the tops of the muffins are suntanned brown. Check that the muffins are cooked through by inserting a cocktail stick into one of them – if it comes out dry, they are ready. Transfer them from the muffin tray to a wire rack, place on their sides and allow to cool completely before serving.

STICKY MANGO RICE

1 tablespoon sesame seeds
1 tablespoon desiccated
    coconut
2 cups of black glutinous rice
    (swapsies: white glutinous
    rice) (I use a 240ml/8½fl oz
    cup, holding 195g/7oz rice)
5 cups (see above) of water
1 teaspoon fine sea salt
180ml (6fl oz) coconut milk
2 very ripe mangoes, stoned,
    peeled and sliced

SYRUP
100g (3½oz) palm sugar
    (swapsies: soft brown sugar)
160ml (5½fl oz) water

I love that you can walk down any street in Thailand and know that you are never too far away from a delicious dessert, such as this superior rice pudding. And happily it's something you can easily reproduce back home. I would eat this when the rice is still warm with super-ripe mangoes, but it can also be served chilled and you can vary it by using white glutinous rice instead of black rice too. Coconut and mango work so well together that I sometimes wonder why they don't grow from the same tree!

1. Mix the syrup ingredients together in a small saucepan and bring to a boil, then reduce the heat to medium and simmer for 20 minutes until it reaches the consistency of maple syrup.

2. Meanwhile, toast the sesame seeds and desiccated coconut together in a dry frying pan on a medium heat for about 5 minutes, stirring and tossing, until uniformly golden brown. Transfer to a bowl.

3. Cover the rice in cold water (about a 4:1 ratio of water to rice) and leave to soak for at least 3 hours. Then pour the rice through a sieve to drain. Wash the rice up to 5 times. Place in a bowl and run under cold water, gently moving the rice grains between the tips of your fingers. The excess starch from the rice grains will initially make the water quite cloudy, so pour the rice through a sieve in between each wash. By the end of washing, the water should run clear.

4. Sieve the rice one last time and place it in a saucepan with the measured water, 2 tablespoons of the syrup and the salt. Bring to a boil, then reduce the heat to medium and cook for 30–35 minutes, stirring every 5 minutes, until the rice is cooked through and looks like thick wet porridge. Remove from the heat and allow to cool for about 20 minutes before serving.

5. To serve, divide the rice between 6 bowls, pour 2 tablespoons of the coconut milk over each, add the sliced mangoes and then finish each bowl off with a drizzle of the syrup and the toasted sesame seeds and desiccated coconut.

D
E
S
S
E
R
T
S

199

JAPANESE SOUFFLÉ CHEESECAKE

CHEESE MIXTURE
230g (8oz) cream cheese
60g (2¼oz) unsalted butter,
   plus 1 tablespoon for greasing
50g (1¾oz) caster sugar
1 teaspoon vanilla extract

BATTER
130ml (4½fl oz) full-fat milk
5 egg yolks
40g (1½oz) plain flour, sifted
20g (¾oz) cornflour, sifted

MERINGUE
5 egg whites
¼ teaspoon cream of tartar
50g (1¾oz) caster sugar

TO SERVE
icing sugar, for dusting
   (optional)
raspberries (optional)

NOTE
If you only have a springform
cake tin, then wrap the outside
of the tin in aluminium foil
before starting, to prevent the
water leaking into the cake.
If you do happen to have any
leftovers of this, make sure you
keep them in the fridge because
of the high cheese content.

Achieving a Japanese cheesecake's fluffy texture is an exacting process, perhaps better described as reforging a long-lost friendship with your oven to fathom where, if any, its hot spots are. If you happen to get any crinkles or cracks on top, just dust 2 tablespoons of icing sugar over to hide the imperfections – your friends will be equally wowed and everyone will want more than one slice once they start to dig in!

1. Rub the 1 tablespoon of butter around the inside of a 20cm (8 inch) round nonstick cake tin with kitchen paper. Cut 2 long, 5cm (2 inch) wide, strips of baking paper and place to form a cross inside the tin with the ends overhanging the edges with which to lift the baked cheesecake out. Cut a circle of baking paper for the base and a strip for the edge and use to line the cake tin.

2. Stir the cheese mixture ingredients together in a saucepan on a low heat for 3–4 minutes, until smooth. Allow to cool.

3. Preheat the oven to 165°C/360°F/Gas Mark 4½. Whisk the batter ingredients together gently in a mixing bowl until well combined. Add the cheese mixture a ladle at a time and whisk in gently until the batter looks like custard.

4. For the meringue, place the egg whites and cream of tartar in a large, very clean mixing bowl and whisk until soft peaks form. Then add the caster sugar, 1 tablespoon at a time, whisking well after each addition. Whisk until stiff and silky smooth. Gradually fold 2 tablespoons of meringue into the batter. Repeat 4 times. Add the remaining meringue to the batter and incorporate gently, trying to lose as little air as possible.

5. Fill a deep roasting tray halfway with boiling water and place in the oven. Pour the cake mixture into the lined cake tin, stand in the hot water and bake for 25 minutes. Reduce the temperature to 120°C/275°F/Gas Mark 1 and open the oven door for 30 seconds. Close the door and bake for another hour. Turn the oven off, open the oven door for 5 minutes, then wedge the door open to allow the cake to cool slowly for another hour. Remove from the oven, then remove the cake tin from the water. Carefully lift the cheesecake out of the tin using the paper strips.

CANNED FRUIT ICE KACANG

2 x c.415g (14½oz) cans of
    peaches in juice or light syrup
2 x c.415g (14½oz) cans of
    summer fruits in juice
    or light syrup
2 x c.565g (1lb 4oz) cans of
    lychees in juice or light syrup
2–3 tablespoons condensed milk
    or 150ml (5fl oz) coconut milk
    and 1 tablespoon palm sugar
    (swapsies: soft brown sugar)

GRANITA
(Quantities per fruit flavour)
250g (9oz) canned fruit
    pieces from above, juice
    squeezed out
1 tablespoon caster sugar
4 tablespoons water
1 teaspoon lemon juice

JELLY
(Quantites per fruit flavour)
240ml (8½fl oz) juice or light
    syrup reserved from the
    canned fruits above
½ tablespoon agar agar flakes

SUGGESTED TOPPINGS
½ x c.420g (14¾oz) can of
    creamed-style sweetcorn
½ x 400g (14oz) can of kidney
    beans, drained
fresh strawberries
any fruits leftover from the cans

Ice *kacang* is a street-food shaved ice that every Malaysian I know seems to have a designated space for in their tummies, no matter how full they are. It's hard to make perfectly shaved ice and all the accompanying syrups at home, but I've come up with a simple way to knock up a cheap and cheerful dessert that everyone will love. I suggest you mix and match your fruit and toppings, using the granita and jelly quantities as your guide to achieving the right texture and flavour balance. You will need a full day to complete the preparations so make sure to plan ahead.

1. Strain each of the canned fruits separately through a sieve set over a jug or bowl to catch the juice or syrup, reserving the juice or syrup to make the jellies. Place the measured amount of the peaches in a food processor or smoothie maker along with the rest of the granita ingredients and blitz until smooth. Remove from the processor and repeat with the canned summer fruits, then with the canned lychees.

2. Pour each granita mixture into a separate shallow roasting tray that will fit into your freezer. Freeze, uncovered, for 40 minutes. Remove the trays from the freezer and use a fork to break up any frozen granita to create a uniform slush, then return to the freezer. Repeat this process 4–5 times over the course of the day.

3. Mix the jelly ingredients in a saucepan and bring to a boil. (For peaches, I recommend spooning in 3–4 tablespoons of the peach granita before boiling to make it more colourful.) Reduce the heat to low and simmer for 5–10 minutes until the agar agar dissolves. Cool and refrigerate overnight in an airtight container.

4. If using coconut milk, mix the coconut milk and palm sugar together in a saucepan. Bring to a boil until the sugar has melted. Allow to cool, then chill in the fridge for at least 1 hour.

5. When ready to serve, spoon out a heap of each granita, then cut the jellies into whatever shape you wish and add it to the granita. Top the granita with the condensed milk or sweetened coconut milk and then add toppings of your choice, depending on how traditional you want to go with your ice *kacang*!

INDEX

GLOSSARY

UK

UK	US
aubergine	eggplant
baby sweetcorn	baby corn
baking paper	parchment paper
barbecued	grilled
beef shin	beef shank
birds' eye chilli	Thai chili pepper
blitz	process/blend
caster sugar	superfine sugar
cavolo nero	Tuscan kale
chilli flakes	crushed red pepper flakes
chips	fries
coriander leaves/stalks/roots	cilantro leaves/stems/roots (but coriander seed)
cornflour	cornstarch
desiccated coconut	unsweetened desiccated coconut or substitute unsweetened shredded coconut
double cream	heavy cream
fish sauce	Thai fish sauce
full-fat milk	whole milk
gherkins	pickles
grill/grill rack	broil or broiler/broiler rack
hob	stove
icing sugar	confectioners' sugar
instant oats	instant oatmeal
jug	pitcher/liquid measuring jug
kecap manis	sweet soy sauce
kitchen paper	paper towels
lemonade	lemon-flavored soda pop
mangetout	snow peas
minced (meat)	ground (meat)
moreish	something so delicious that it's hard to stop eating it
muffin cases	muffin liners
pak choi	bok choy
plain flour	all-purpose flour
prawns (tiger)	shrimp (jumbo)
semi-skimmed milk	low-fat milk
Shaoxing rice wine	Chinese rice wine
sieve	strainer
single cream	light cream
soft brown sugar	light brown sugar
spring onions	scallions
starter	appetizer
stock	broth
stoned	pitted
sugarsnaps	snow peas
sweetcorn cobs	corncobs or ears of corn
sweetheart cabbage	a pointed green cabbage, also known as hispi cabbage
takeaway	takeout
tea towel	dish towel
Tenderstem broccoli	baby broccoli or Broccolini
tomato purée	tomato paste

ACKNOWLEDGEMENTS

Thanks to Eleanor Maxfield and the whole Octopus team, for believing in me; Richard Watts, the kindest, most thoughtful agent in the world; Pauline Bache for helping me decipher the feasting code; Adrienne Katz Kennedy for once again being a friendly ⟨…⟩ that I passed in the night; Jaz Bahra for ⟨…⟩ sharp eye and keeping Kris Kirkham in ⟨…⟩ Kris Kirkham, for making the food JUM⟨…⟩ at us all; Phoebe Pearson and Laura Be⟨…⟩ for also keeping Kris in check; Morag ⟨…⟩ Farquhar for the beautiful cutlery and ⟨…⟩ Yasmin Othman and Gileng Salter my ⟨…⟩ yet super-efficient Food Stylo Milos; ⟨…⟩ Herft for kickstarting some of the f⟨…⟩ Natalia Middleton for her kitchen-ca⟨…⟩ Freya Deabill from The Brand New S⟨…⟩ again, for such wonderful, on point ⟨…⟩ illustrations; and Emma and Alex fro⟨…⟩ Smith & Gilmour, for making the de⟨…⟩ so perfectly aligned.

A night out with the School of Wok te⟨…⟩ always reminds me how lucky I am to b⟨…⟩ surrounded by such a passionate and ca⟨…⟩ team, in which each new addition adds ⟨…⟩ another song to the ever-growing karaoke ⟨…⟩ Nev Leaning, Yolanda Ocon Andrew, Clare ⟨…⟩ Cassidy-Sefati, Chris Jackson, Lee Skillett, Arthur Barker, Hannah Dryden-Jones, Michelle Chau, Beverley Benn, Cher Loh, Ryan Yen, Ian Carter, Ethan Kayem, Lesley Gane, Ben Marson and Max Rees, I thank you all for being so sing-your-heart-out dedicated to our beloved School of Wok.